Learn Python in One Day and Learn It Well
Python for Beginners with Hands-on Project
The only book you need to start coding in Python immediately
(Second Edition)

By Jamie Chan

http://www.learncodingfast.com/python

Copyright © 2014; 2017

Preface

This book is written to help you learn Python programming FAST and learn it WELL. If you are an absolute beginner in Programming, you'll find that this book explains complex concepts in an easy to understand manner. If you are an experienced coder, this book gives you a good base from which to explore Python.

Topics are carefully selected to give you a broad exposure to Python, while not overwhelming you with information overload. These topics include control structures, error handling techniques, file handling techniques and more. New chapters on object-oriented programming are also included in this edition.

Examples are carefully chosen to demonstrate each concept so that you can gain a deeper understand of the language. The appendices at the end of the book will also provide you with a convenient reference for some of the commonly used functions in Python.

In addition, as Richard Branson puts it: "The best way of learning about anything is by doing". At the end of the course, you'll be guided through a project that gives you a chance to put what you've learned to use.

You can download the source code for the project and the appendices at http://www.learncodingfast.com/python

Any errata can be found at
http://www.learncodingfast.com/errata

Contact Information

I would love to hear from you.
For feedback or queries, you can contact me at
jamie@learncodingfast.com.

More Books by Jamie

C#: Learn C# in One Day and Learn It Well

Java: Learn Java in One Day and Learn It Well

CSS: Learn CSS in One Day and Learn It Well

Table of Contents

Chapter 1: Python, what Python?

Welcome to the exciting world of programming. I'm so glad you picked up this book and I sincerely hope this book can help you master the Python language and experience the exhilaration of programming. Before we dive into the nuts and bolts of Python programming, let us first answer a few questions.

1.1 What is Python?

Python is a widely used high-level programming language created by Guido van Rossum in the late 1980s. The language places strong emphasis on code readability and simplicity, making it possible for programmers to develop applications rapidly.

Like all high level programming languages, Python code resembles the English language which computers are unable to understand. Codes that we write in Python have to be interpreted by a special program known as the Python interpreter, which we'll have to install before we can code, test and execute our Python programs. We'll look at how to install the Python interpreter in Chapter 2.

There are also a number of third-party tools, such as Py2exe or Pyinstaller that allow us to package our Python code into stand-alone executable programs for some of the most popular operating systems like Windows and Mac OS. This allows us to distribute our Python programs without requiring the users to install the Python interpreter.

1.2 Why Learn Python?

There are a large number of high level programming languages available, such as C, C++, and Java. The good news is all high level programming languages are very similar to one another. What differs is mainly the syntax, the libraries available and the way we access those libraries. A library is simply a collection of resources and pre-written codes that we can use when we write our programs. If you learn one language well, you can easily learn a new language in a fraction of the time it took you to learn the first language.

If you are new to programming, Python is a great place to start. One of the key features of Python is its simplicity, making it the ideal language for beginners to learn. Most programs in Python require considerably fewer lines of code to perform the same task compared to other languages such as C. This leads to fewer programming errors and reduces the development time needed. In addition, Python comes with an extensive collection of third party resources that extend the capabilities of the language. As such, Python can be used for a large variety of tasks, such as for desktop applications, database applications, network programming, game programming and even mobile development. Last but not least, Python is a cross platform language, which means that code written for one operating system, such as Windows, will work well on Mac OS or Linux without making any changes to the Python code.

Convinced that Python is THE language to learn? Let's get started...

Chapter 2: Getting ready for Python

2.1 Installing the Interpreter

Before we can write our first Python program, we have to download the appropriate interpreter for our computers.

We'll be using Python 3 in this book because as stated on the official Python site "Python 2.x is legacy, Python 3.x is the present and future of the language". In addition, "Python 3 eliminates many quirks that can unnecessarily trip up beginning programmers".

However, note that Python 2 is currently still rather widely used. Python 2 and 3 are about 90% similar. Hence if you learn Python 3, you will likely have no problems understanding codes written in Python 2.

To install the interpreter for Python 3, head over to https://www.python.org/downloads/. The correct version should be indicated at the top of the webpage. We'll be using version 3.6.1 in this book. Click on "Download Python 3.6.1" and the software will start downloading.

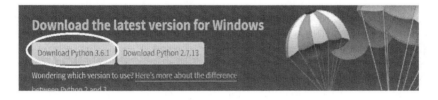

Alternatively if you want to install a different version, scroll down the page and you'll see a listing of other versions. Click on the release version that you want. You'll be redirected to the download page for that version.

Scroll down towards the end of the page and you'll see a table listing various installers for that version. Choose the correct installer for your computer. The installer to use depends on two factors:

1. The operating system (Windows, Mac OS, or Linux) and
2. The processor (32-bit vs 64-bit) that you are using.

For instance, if you are using a 64-bit Windows computer, you will likely be using the "**Windows** x86-**64** executable installer". Just click on the link to download it. If you download and run the wrong installer, no worries. You will get an error message and the interpreter will not install. Simply download the correct installer and you are good to go.

Once you have successfully installed the interpreter, you are ready to start coding in Python.

2.2 Using the Python Shell, IDLE and Writing our FIRST program

We'll be writing our code using the IDLE program that comes bundled with our Python interpreter.

To do that, let's first launch the IDLE program. You launch the IDLE program like how you launch any other programs. For instance on Windows 10, you can search for it by typing "IDLE" in the search box. Once it is found, click on IDLE (Python GUI) to launch it. You'll be presented with the Python Shell shown below.

The Python Shell allows us to use Python in interactive mode. This means we can enter one command at a time. The Shell waits for a command from the user, executes it and returns the result of the execution. After this, the Shell waits for the next command.

Try typing the following into the Shell. The lines starting with >>> are the commands you should type while the lines after the commands show the results.

```
>>> 2+3
5
>>> 3>2
True
>>> print ('Hello World')
Hello World
```

When you type 2+3, you are issuing a command to the Shell, asking it to evaluate the value of 2+3. Hence, the Shell returns the answer 5. When you type 3>2, you are asking the Shell if 3 is greater than 2. The Shell replies True. Next, print is a command asking the Shell to display the line Hello World.

The Python Shell is a very convenient tool for testing Python commands, especially when we are first getting started with the language. However, if you exit from the Python Shell and enter it again, all the commands you type will be gone. In addition, you cannot use the Python Shell to create an actual program. To code an actual program, you need to write your code in a text file and save it with a .py extension. This file is known as a Python script.

To create a Python script, click on File > New File in the top menu of our Python Shell. This will bring up the text editor that we are going to use to write our very first program, the "Hello World" program. Writing the "Hello World" program is kind of like the rite of passage for all new programmers. We'll be using this program to familiarize ourselves with the IDLE software.

Type the following code into the text editor (not the Shell).

```
#Prints the Words "Hello World"
print ("Hello World")
```

You should notice that the line `#Prints the Words "Hello World"` is in red while the word `print` is in purple and `"Hello World"` is in green. This is the software's way of making our code easier to read. The words `print` and `"Hello World"` serve different purposes in our program, hence they are displayed using different colors. We'll go into more details in later chapters.

The line `#Prints the Words "Hello World"` (in red) is actually not part of the program. It is a comment written to make our code more readable for other programmers. This line is ignored by the Python interpreter. To add comments to our program, we type a # sign in front of each line of comment, like this:

```
#This is a comment
#This is also a comment
#This is yet another comment
```

Alternatively, we can also use three single quotes (or three double quotes) for multiline comments, like this:

```
'''
This is a comment
This is also a comment
This is yet another comment
'''
```

Now click File > Save As... to save your code. Make sure you save it with the .py extension.

Done? Voilà! You have just successfully written your first Python program.

Finally click on Run > Run Module to execute the program (or press F5). You should see the words `Hello World` printed on your Python Shell.

Chapter 3: The World of Variables and Operators

Now that we're done with the introductory stuff, let's get down to the real stuff. In this chapter, you'll learn all about variables and operators. Specifically, you'll learn what variables are and how to name and declare them. We'll also learn about the common operations that we can perform on them. Ready? Let's go.

3.1 What are variables?

Variables are names given to data that we need to store and manipulate in our programs. For instance, suppose your program needs to store the age of a user. To do that, we can name this data `userAge` and define the variable `userAge` using the following statement.

```
userAge = 0
```

After you define the variable `userAge`, your program will allocate a certain area of your computer's storage space to store this data. You can then access and modify this data by referring to it by its name, `userAge`. Every time you declare a new variable, you need to give it an initial value. In this example, we gave it the value 0. We can always change this value in our program later.

We can also define multiple variables at one go. To do that simply write

```
userAge, userName = 30, 'Peter'
```

This is equivalent to

```
userAge = 30
userName = 'Peter'
```

3.2 Naming a Variable

A variable name in Python can only contain letters (a - z, A - B), numbers or underscores (_). However, the first character cannot be a number. Hence, you can name your variables `userName`, `user_name` or `userName2` but not `2userName`.

In addition, there are some reserved words that you cannot use as a variable name because they already have preassigned meanings in Python. These reserved words include words like `print`, `input`, `if`, `while` etc. We'll learn about each of them in subsequent chapters.

Finally, variable names are case sensitive. `username` is not the same as `userName`.

There are two conventions when naming a variable in Python. We can either use the camel case notation or use underscores. Camel case is the practice of writing compound words with mixed casing (e.g. `thisIsAVariableName`). This is the convention that we'll be using in the rest of the book. Alternatively, another common practice is to use underscores (_) to separate the words. If you prefer, you can name your variables like this: `this_is_a_variable_name`.

3.3 The Assignment Operator

Note that the = sign in the statement `userAge = 0` has a different meaning from the = sign we learned in Math. In programming, the = sign is known as an assignment operator. It means we are assigning the value on the right side of the = sign to the variable on the left. A good way to understand the statement `userAge = 0` is to *think of it* as `userAge <- 0`.

The statements `x = y` and `y = x` have very different meanings in programming.

Confused? An example will likely clear this up.

Type the following code into your IDLE editor and save it.

```
x = 5
y = 10
x = y
print ("x = ", x)
print ("y = ", y)
```

Now run the program. You should get this output:

```
x = 10
y = 10
```

Although x has an initial value of 5 (declared on the first line), the third line $x = y$ assigns the value of y to x (think of it as $x <- y$), hence changing the value of x to 10 while the value of y remains unchanged.

Next, modify the program by changing ONLY ONE statement: Change the third line from $x = y$ to $y = x$. Mathematically, $x = y$ and $y = x$ mean the same thing. However, this is not so in programming.

Run the second program. You will now get

```
x = 5
y = 5
```

You can see that in this example, the x value remains as 5, but the value of y is changed to 5. This is because the statement $y = x$ assigns the value of x to y.

y becomes 5 while x remains unchanged as 5.

3.4 Basic Operators

Besides assigning a variable an initial value, we can also perform the usual mathematical operations on variables. Basic operators in Python include +, -, *, /, //, % and ** which represent addition, subtraction, multiplication, division, floor division, modulus and exponent respectively.

Example:

Suppose x = 5, y = 2

Addition:
```
x + y = 7
```

Subtraction:
```
x - y = 3
```

Multiplication:
```
x*y = 10
```

Division:
```
x/y = 2.5
```

Floor Division:
```
x//y = 2
```
(rounds down the answer to the nearest whole number)

Modulus:
```
x%y = 1
```
(gives the remainder when 5 is divided by 2)

Exponent:
```
x**y = 25
```
(5 to the power of 2)

3.5 More Assignment Operators

Besides the = operator, there are a few more assignment operators in Python (and most programming languages). These include operators like +=, -= and *=.

Suppose we have the variable x, with an initial value of 10. If we want to increment x by 2, we can write

```
x = x + 2
```

The program will <u>first evaluate the expression on the right</u> (x + 2) and assign the answer to the left. So eventually the statement above becomes x = 12.

Instead of writing x = x + 2, we can also write x += 2 to express the same meaning. The += sign is actually a shorthand that combines the assignment sign with the addition operator. Hence, x += 2 simply means x = x + 2.

Similarly, if we want to do a subtraction, we can write x = x - 2 or x -= 2. The same works for all the 7 operators mentioned in the section above.

Chapter 4: Data Types in Python

Now, let us move on to look at data types in Python. Data type simply refers to the type of data that a variable stores.

We'll first look at some basic data types in Python, specifically the integer, float and string. Next, we'll explore the concept of type casting. Finally, we'll discuss three more advanced data types in Python: the list, tuple and dictionary.

4.1 Integers

Integers are numbers with no decimal parts, such as -5, -4, -3, 0, 5, 7 etc.

To declare an integer in Python, simply write `variableName = initial value`

Example:
```
userAge = 20
mobileNumber = 12398724
```

4.2 Float

Float refers to numbers that have decimal parts, such as 1.234, -0.023, 12.01.

To declare a float in Python, we write `variableName = initial value`

Example:
```
userHeight = 1.82
userWeight = 67.2
```

4.3 String

String refers to text.

To declare a string, you can either use `variableName = 'initial value'` (single quotes) or `variableName = "initial value"` (double quotes)

Example:
```
userName = 'Peter'
userSpouseName = "Janet"
userAge = '30'
```

In the last example, because we wrote `userAge = '30'`, `userAge` is a string. In contrast, if you wrote `userAge = 30` (without quotes), `userAge` is an integer.

We can combine multiple substrings by using the concatenate sign (+). For instance, `"Peter " + "Lee"` is equivalent to the string `"Peter Lee"`.

Built-In String Functions

Python includes a number of built-in functions to manipulate strings. A function is a block of reusable code that performs a certain task. We'll discuss functions in greater depth in Chapter 7.

An example of a function available in Python is the `upper()` method for strings. You use it to capitalize all the letters in a string. For instance, `'Peter'.upper()` will give us the string `'PETER'`. You can refer to Appendix A for more examples and sample codes on how to use Python's built-in string methods.

Formatting Strings using the % Operator

Strings can also be formatted using the % operator. This gives you greater control over how you want your string to be displayed and stored. The syntax for using the % operator is

```
"string to be formatted" %(values or variables
to be inserted into string, separated by commas)
```

There are three parts to this syntax. First we write the string to be formatted in quotes. Next we write the % symbol. Finally, we have a pair of parentheses ( ) within which we write the values or variables to be inserted into the string. This parentheses with values inside is actually known as a tuple, a data type that we'll cover later in this chapter.

Type the following code in IDLE and run it.

```
brand = 'Apple'

exchangeRate = 1.235235245

message = 'The price of this %s laptop is %d USD
and the exchange rate is %4.2f USD to 1
EUR' %(brand, 1299, exchangeRate)

print (message)
```

In the example above, the string `'The price of this %s laptop is %d USD and the exchange rate is %4.2f USD to 1 EUR'` is the string that we want to format.

`%s`, `%d` and `%4.2f` are known as formatters; they serve as placeholders in the string.

These placeholders will be replaced with the variable `brand`, the value 1299 and the variable `exchangeRate` respectively, as indicated in the parentheses. If we run the code, we'll get the output below.

```
The price of this Apple laptop is 1299 USD and
the exchange rate is 1.24 USD to 1 EUR
```

The `%s` formatter is used to represent a string (`'Apple'` in this case) while the `%d` formatter represents an integer (1299). If we want to add spaces before an integer, we can add a number between `%` and `d` to indicate the desired length of the string. For instance `"%5d" % (123)` will give us `"  123"` (with 2 spaces in front and a total length of 5).

The `%f` formatter is used to format floats (numbers with decimals). Here we format it as `%4.2f` where 4 refers to the total length and 2 refers to 2 decimal places. If we want to add spaces before the number, we can format is as `%7.2f`, which will give us `"   1.24"` (with 2 decimal places, 3 spaces in front and a total length of 7).

Formatting Strings using the `format()` method

In addition to using the `%` operator to format strings, Python also provides us with the `format()` method to format strings. The syntax is

```
"string to be formatted".format(values or
variables to be inserted into string, separated
by commas)
```

When we use the `format()` method, we do not use `%s`, `%f` or `%d` as placeholders. Instead we use braces { }, like this:

```
message = 'The price of this {0:s} laptop is
{1:d} USD and the exchange rate is {2:4.2f} USD
to 1 EUR'.format('Apple', 1299, 1.235235245)
```

Inside the braces, we first write the position of the argument to use, followed by a colon. After the colon, we write the formatter. There should not be any spaces within the braces.

When we write `format('Apple', 1299, 1.235235245)`, we are passing in three arguments to the `format()` method. Arguments are data that the method needs in order to perform its task. The arguments are `'Apple'`, `1299` and `1.235235245`.

The argument `'Apple'` has a position of 0,
`1299` has a position of 1 and
`1.235235245` has a position of 2.

Positions always start from ZERO.

When we write `{0:s}`, we are asking the interpreter to replace `{0:s}` with the argument in position 0 and that it is a string (because the formatter is `s`).

When we write `{1:d}`, we are referring to the argument in position 1, which is an integer (formatter is `d`).

When we write `{2:4.2f}`, we are referring to the argument in position 2, which is a float and we want it to be formatted with 2 decimal places and a total length of 4 (formatter is `4.2f`).

If we print `message`, we'll get
```
The price of this Apple laptop is 1299 USD and
the exchange rate is 1.24 USD to 1 EUR
```

Note: If you do not want to format the string, you can simply write

```
message = 'The price of this {} laptop is {} USD
and the exchange rate is {} USD to 1
EUR'.format('Apple', 1299, 1.235235245)
```

Here we do not have to specify the position of the arguments. The interpreter will replace the braces based on the order of the arguments provided. We'll get

```
The price of this Apple laptop is 1299 USD and
the exchange rate is 1.235235245 USD to 1 EUR
```

The `format()` method can be kind of confusing to beginners. In fact, string formatting can be more fanciful than what we've covered here, but what we've covered is sufficient for most purposes. To get a better understanding of the `format()` method, try the following program.

```
message1 = '{0} is easier than
{1}'.format('Python', 'Java')
message2 = '{1} is easier than
{0}'.format('Python', 'Java')
message3 = '{:10.2f} and
{:d}'.format(1.234234234, 12)
message4 = '{}'.format(1.234234234)

print (message1)
#You'll get 'Python is easier than Java'

print (message2)
#You'll get 'Java is easier than Python'

print (message3)
#You'll get '      1.23 and 12'
#You do not need to indicate the positions of
the arguments.

print (message4)
#You'll get '1.234234234'. No formatting is
done.
```

You can use the Python Shell to experiment with the `format()` method. Try typing in various strings and see what you get.

4.4 Type Casting In Python

Sometimes in our program, it is necessary for us to convert from one data type to another, such as from an integer to a string. This is known as type casting.

There are three built-in functions in Python that allow us to do type casting. These are the `int()`, `float()`, and `str()` functions.

The `int()` function in Python takes in a float or an appropriate string and converts it to an integer. To change a float to an integer, we can type `int(5.712987)`. We'll get 5 as the result (anything after the decimal point is removed). To change a string to an integer, we can type `int("4")` and we'll get 4. However, we cannot type `int("Hello")` or `int("4.22321")`. We'll get an error in both cases.

The `float()` function takes in an integer or an appropriate string and changes it to a float. For instance, if we type `float(2)` or `float("2")`, we'll get 2.0. If we type `float("2.09109")`, we'll get 2.09109 which is a float and not a string since the quotation marks are removed.

The `str()` function on the other hand converts an integer or a float to a string. For instance, if we type `str(2.1)`, we'll get "2.1".

Now that we've covered the three basic data types in Python and their casting, let's move on to the more advanced data types.

4.5 List

List refers to a collection of data which are normally related. Instead of storing these data as separate variables, we can store them as a list. For instance, suppose our program needs to store the age of 5 users. Instead of storing them as `user1Age`, user2Age, user3Age, user4Age and user5Age, it makes more sense to store them as a list.

To declare a list, you write listName = [initial values]. Note that we use square brackets [ ] when declaring a list. Multiple values are separated by a comma.

Example:
userAge = [21, 22, 23, 24, 25]

We can also declare a list without assigning any initial values to it. We simply write listName = []. What we have now is an empty list with no items in it. We have to use the append() method mentioned later to add items to the list.

Individual values in the list are accessible by their indexes, and indexes always start from ZERO, not 1. This is a common practice in almost all programming languages, such as C and Java. Hence the first value has an index of 0, the next has an index of 1 and so forth. For instance, userAge[0] = 21, userAge[1] = 22.

Alternatively, you can access the values of a list from the back. The last item in the list has an index of -1, the second last has an index of -2 and so forth. Hence, userAge[-1] = 25, userAge[-2] = 24.

You can assign a list, or part of it, to a variable. If you write userAge2 = userAge, the variable userAge2 becomes [21, 22, 23, 24, 25].

If you write userAge3 = userAge[2:4], you are assigning items with index 2 to index 4-1 from the list userAge to the list userAge3. In other words, userAge3 = [23, 24].

The notation 2:4 is known as a slice. Whenever we use the slice notation in Python, the item at the start index is always included, but <u>the item at the end is always excluded</u>. Hence the notation 2:4 refers to items from index 2 to index 4-1 (i.e. index 3), which is why `userAge3` = `[23, 24]` and not `[23, 24, 25]`.

The slice notation includes a third number known as the stepper. If we write `userAge4 = userAge[1:5:2]`, we will get a sub list consisting of <u>every second number </u>from index 1 to index 5-1 because the stepper is 2. Hence, `userAge4 = [22, 24]`.

In addition, slice notations have useful defaults. The default for the first number is zero, and the default for the second number is size of the list being sliced. For instance, `userAge[ :4]` gives you values from index 0 to index 4-1 while `userAge[1: ]` gives you values from index 1 to index 5-1 (since the size of `userAge` is 5, i.e. `userAge` has 5 items).

To modify items in a list, we write `listName[index of item to be modified] = new value`. For instance, if you want to modify the second item, you write `userAge[1] = 5`. Your list becomes `userAge = [21, 5, 23, 24, 25]`.

To add items, you use the `append()` function. For instance, if you write `userAge.append(99)`, you add the value 99 to the end of the list. Your list is now `userAge = [21, 5, 23, 24, 25, 99]`.

To remove items, you write `del listName[index of item to be deleted]`. For instance, if you write `del userAge[2]`, your list now becomes `userAge = [21, 5, 24, 25, 99]` (the third item is deleted)

To fully appreciate the workings of a list, try running the following program.

```
#declaring the list, list elements can be of
different data types
myList = [1, 2, 3, 4, 5, "Hello"]
```

```python
#print the entire list.
print(myList)
#You'll get [1, 2, 3, 4, 5, "Hello"]

#print the third item (recall: Index starts from
zero).
print(myList[2])
#You'll get 3

#print the last item.
print(myList[-1])
#You'll get "Hello"

#assign myList (from index 1 to 4) to myList2
and print myList2
myList2 = myList[1:5]
print (myList2)
#You'll get [2, 3, 4, 5]

#modify the second item in myList and print the
updated list
myList[1] = 20
print(myList)
#You'll get [1, 20, 3, 4, 5, 'Hello']

#append a new item to myList and print the
updated list
myList.append("How are you")
print(myList)
#You'll get [1, 20, 3, 4, 5, 'Hello', 'How are
you']

#remove the sixth item from myList and print the
updated list
del myList[5]
print(myList)
#You'll get [1, 20, 3, 4, 5, 'How are you']
```

There are a couple more things that you can do with a list. For sample codes and more examples on working with a list, refer to Appendix B.

4.6 Tuple

Tuples are just like lists, but you cannot modify their values. The initial values are the values that will stay for the rest of the program. An example where tuples are useful is when your program needs to store the names of the months of the year.

To declare a tuple, you write `tupleName = (initial values)`. Notice that we use parentheses ( ) when declaring a tuple. Multiple values are separated by a comma.

Example:
```
monthsOfYear = ("Jan", "Feb", "Mar", "Apr",
"May", "Jun", "Jul", "Aug", "Sep", "Oct", "Nov",
"Dec")
```

You access the individual values of a tuple using their indexes, just like with a list.
Hence, `monthsOfYear[0]` = `"Jan"`, `monthsOfYear[-1]` = `"Dec"`.

For more examples of what you can do with a tuple, check out Appendix C.

4.7 Dictionary

Dictionary is a collection of related data PAIRS. For instance, if we want to store the username and age of 5 users, we can store them in a dictionary.

To declare a dictionary, you write `dictionaryName = {dictionary key : data}`, with the requirement that

dictionary keys must be unique (within one dictionary). That is, you should not declare a dictionary like this
`myDictionary = {"Peter":38, "John":51, "Peter":13}.`

This is because "Peter" is used as the dictionary key twice. Note that we use braces { } when declaring a dictionary. Multiple pairs are separated by commas.

Example:
`userNameAndAge = {"Peter":38, "John":51, "Alex":13, "Alvin":"Not Available"}`

You can also declare a dictionary using the `dict( )` method. To declare the `userNameAndAge` dictionary above, you write

`userNameAndAge = dict(Peter = 38, John = 51, Alex = 13, Alvin = "Not Available")`

When you use this method to declare a dictionary, you use parentheses ( ) instead of braces { } and you do not put quotation marks for the dictionary keys.

To access individual items in the dictionary, we use the dictionary key, which is the first value in the `{dictionary key : data}` pair. For instance, to get John's age, you write `userNameAndAge["John"]`. You'll get the value `51`.

To modify items in a dictionary, we write
`dictionaryName[dictionary key of item to be modified] = new data.`

For instance, to modify the `"John":51` pair, we write `userNameAndAge["John"] = 21`. Our dictionary now becomes `userNameAndAge = {"Peter":38, "John":21, "Alex":13, "Alvin":"Not Available"}.`

We can also declare a dictionary without assigning any initial values to it. We simply write `dictionaryName = { }`. What we have now is an empty dictionary with no items in it.

To add items to a dictionary, we write `dictionaryName[dictionary key] = data`. For instance, if we want to add `"Joe":40` to our dictionary, we write `userNameAndAge["Joe"] = 40`. Our dictionary now becomes `userNameAndAge = {"Peter":38, "John":21, "Alex":13, "Alvin":"Not Available", "Joe":40}`

To remove items from a dictionary, we write `del dictionaryName[dictionary key]`. For instance, to remove the `"Alex":13` pair, we write `del userNameAndAge["Alex"]`. Our dictionary now becomes `userNameAndAge = {"Peter":38, "John":21, "Alvin":"Not Available", "Joe":40}`

Run the following program to see all these in action.

```
#declaring the dictionary, dictionary keys and
data can be of different data types
myDict = {"One":1.35, 2.5:"Two Point Five",
3:"+", 7.9:2}

#print the entire dictionary
print(myDict)
#You'll get {'One': 1.35, 2.5: 'Two Point Five',
3: '+', 7.9: 2}
#Items may be displayed in a different order
#Items in a dictionary are not necessarily
stored in the same order as the way you declared
them.

#print the item with key = "One".
print(myDict["One"])
#You'll get 1.35
```

```
#print the item with key = 7.9.
print(myDict[7.9])
#You'll get 2

#modify the item with key = 2.5 and print the
updated dictionary
myDict[2.5] = "Two and a Half"
print(myDict)
#You'll get {'One': 1.35, 2.5: 'Two and a Half',
3: '+', 7.9: 2}

#add a new item and print the updated dictionary
myDict["New item"] = "I'm new"
print(myDict)
#You'll get {'One': 1.35, 2.5: 'Two and a Half',
3: '+', 7.9: 2, 'New item': 'I'm new'}

#remove the item with key = "One" and print the
updated dictionary
del myDict["One"]
print(myDict)
#You'll get {2.5: 'Two and a Half', 3: '+', 7.9:
2, 'New item': 'I'm new'}
```

For more examples and sample codes of working with a dictionary, you can refer to Appendix D.

Chapter 5: Making Your Program Interactive

Now that we've covered the basics of variables, let us write a program that makes use of them. We'll revisit the "Hello World" program we wrote in Chapter 2, but this time we'll make it interactive. Instead of just saying hello to the world, we want the world to know our names and ages too. In order to do that, our program needs to be able to prompt us for information and display them on the screen.

Two built-in functions can do that for us: `input()` and `print()`.

For now, let's type the following program in IDLE. Save it and run it.

```
myName = input("Please enter your name: ")
myAge = input("What about your age: ")

print ("Hello World, my name is", myName, "and I
am", myAge, "years old.")
```

The program should prompt you for your name.

```
Please enter your name:
```

Supposed you entered James. Now press Enter and it'll prompt you for your age.

```
What about your age:
```

Say you keyed in 20. Now press Enter again. You should get the following statement:

```
Hello World, my name is James and I am 20 years
old.
```

5.1 input()

In the example above, we used the `input()` function twice to get our user's name and age.

```
myName = input("Please enter your name: ")
```

The string `"Please enter your name: "` is the prompt that will be displayed on the screen to give instructions to the user. Here, we used a simple string as the prompt. If you prefer, you can use the `%` formatter or the `format()` method discussed in Chapter 4 to format the input string. We'll look at two examples later.

After the prompt is displayed on the screen, the function waits for the user to enter the relevant information. This information is then stored **as a string** in the variable `myName`. The next input statement prompts the user for his age and stores the information **as a string** in the variable `myAge`.

That's how the `input()` function works. Pretty straightforward right?

As mentioned above, in addition to using a simple string as the prompt, we can also use the % formatter or the `format()` method to display the prompt. For instance, we can change the second input statement above from

```
myAge = input("What about your age: ")
```

to

```
myAge = input("Hi %s, what about your age: " %(myName))
```

or

```
myAge = input("Hi {}, what about your age:
".format(myName))
```

We'll get

```
Hi James, what about your age:
```

as the prompt instead.

Note that the `input()` function differs slightly in Python 2 and Python 3. In Python 2, if you want to accept user input as a string, you have to use the `raw_input()` function. The `raw_input()` function works similar to the `input()` function in Python 3.

5.2 print()

Now, let's move on to the `print()` function. The `print()` function is used to display information to users. It accepts zero or more expressions as arguments, separated by commas.

In the statement below, we passed 5 arguments to the `print()` function. Can you identify them?

```
print ("Hello World, my name is", myName, "and I
am", myAge, "years old.")
```

The first is the string `"Hello World, my name is"`
The next is the variable `myName` declared using the `input()` function earlier.
Next is the string `"and I am"`, followed by the variable `myAge` and finally the string `"years old."`.

Note that we do not use quotation marks when referring to the variables `myName` and `myAge`. If you use quotation marks, you'll get the output

```
Hello World, my name is myName and I am myAge
years old.
```

instead, which is obviously not what we want.

Another way to print a statement with variables is to use the % formatter we learned in Chapter 4. To achieve the same output as the first print statement above, we can write

```
print ("Hello World, my name is %s and I am %s
years old." %(myName, myAge))
```

Finally, to print the same statement using the `format()` method, we write

```
print ("Hello World, my name is {} and I am {}
years old".format(myName, myAge))
```

The `print()` function is another function that differs in Python 2 and Python 3. In Python 2, you'll write it without brackets, like this:

```
print "Hello World, my name is " + myName + "
and I am " + myAge + " years old."
```

5.3 Triple Quotes

In some cases, we may want to display a long message using the `print()` function. To do that, we can use the triple-quote symbol ("' or """) to span our message over multiple lines. For instance,

```
print ('''Hello World.
My name is James and
I am 20 years old.''')
```

will give us

```
Hello World.
My name is James and
I am 20 years old.
```

This helps to increase the readability of your message.

5.4 Escape Characters

Sometimes we may also need to print some special "unprintable" characters such as a tab or a newline. In this case, we need to use the \ (backslash) character to escape characters that otherwise have a different meaning.

For instance to print a tab, we type the backslash character before the letter t, like this: `\t`. Without the \ character, the letter t will be printed. With it, a tab is printed. Hence, if you type `print ('Hello\tWorld')`, you'll get `Hello        World`

Other common uses of the backslash character are shown below.
>>> shows the command and the following lines show the output.

<u>\n (Prints a newline)</u>

```
>>> print ('Hello\nWorld')
Hello
World
```

<u>\\ (Prints the backslash character itself)</u>

```
>>> print ('\\')
\
```

<u>\" (Prints double quote, so that the double quote does not signal the end of the string)</u>

```
>>> print ("I am 5'9\" tall")
I am 5'9" tall
```

<u>\' (Print single quote, so that the single quote does not signal the end of the string)</u>

```
>>> print ('I am 5\'9" tall')
I am 5'9" tall
```

If you do not want characters preceded by the \ character to be interpreted as special characters, you can use raw strings by adding an r before the first quote. For instance, if you do not want \t to be interpreted as a tab, you should type print (r'Hello\tWorld'). You will get Hello\tWorld as the output.

Chapter 6: Making Choices and Decisions

Congratulations, you've made it to the most interesting chapter. I hope you've enjoyed the course so far. In this chapter, we'll look at how to make your program smarter, capable of making choices and decisions. Specifically, we'll be looking at the `if` statement, `for` loop and `while` loop. These are known as control flow tools; they control the flow of the program. In addition, we'll also look at the `try, except` statement that determines what the program should do when an error occurs.

However, before we go into these control flow tools, we have to first look at condition statements.

6.1 Condition Statements

All control flow tools involve evaluating a condition statement. The program will proceed differently depending on whether the condition is met.

The most common condition statement is the comparison statement. If we want to compare whether two variables are the same, we use the `==` operator (double `=`). For instance, if you write $x == y$, you are asking the program to check if the value of x is equal to the value of y. If they are equal, the condition is met and the statement will evaluate to `True`. Else, the statement will evaluate to `False`.

Other comparison operators include `!=` (not equal), `<` (smaller than), `>` (greater than), `<=` (smaller than or equal to) and `>=` (greater than or equal to). The list below shows how these signs can be used and gives examples of statements that will evaluate to `True`.

Not equal:
```
5 != 2
```

Greater than:
```
5>2
```

Smaller than:
```
2<5
```

Greater than or equal to:
```
5>=2
5>=5
```

Smaller than or equal to:
```
2 <= 5
2 <= 2
```

We also have three logical operators, `and`, `or`, `not` that are useful if we want to combine multiple conditions.

The `and` operator returns `True` if all conditions are met. Else it will return `False`. For instance, the statement `5==5 and 2>1` will return `True` since both conditions are `True`.

The `or` operator returns `True` if <u>at least one</u> condition is met. Else it will return `False`. The statement `5 > 2 or 7 > 10 or 3 == 2` will return `True` since the first condition `5>2` is `True`.

The `not` operator returns `True` if the condition after the `not` keyword is false. Else it will return `False`. The statement `not 2>5` will return `True` since 2 is not greater than 5.

6.2 If Statement

The `if` statement is one of the most commonly used control flow statements. It allows the program to evaluate if a certain condition is met, and to perform the appropriate action based on the result of the evaluation. The structure of an `if` statement is as follows:

```
if condition 1 is met:
    do A
elif condition 2 is met:
    do B
elif condition 3 is met:
    do C
elif condition 4 is met:
    do D
else:
    do E
```

`elif` stands for "else if" and you can have as many `elif` statements as you like.

If you've coded in other languages like C or Java before, you may be surprised to notice that no parentheses ( ) are needed in Python after the `if`, `elif` and `else` keyword. In addition, Python does not use braces { } to define the start and end of the `if` statement. Rather, Python uses indentation. Anything indented is treated as a block of code that will be executed if the condition evaluates to `True`.

To fully understand how the `if` statement works, fire up IDLE and key in the following code.

```
userInput = input('Enter 1 or 2: ')

if userInput == "1":
    print ("Hello World")
    print ("How are you?")
elif userInput == "2":
    print ("Python Rocks!")
    print ("I love Python")
else:
    print ("You did not enter a valid number")
```

The program first prompts the user for an input using the `input()` function. The result is stored in the `userInput` variable as a string.

Next the statement `if userInput == "1":` compares the `userInput` variable with the string "1". If the value stored in `userInput` is "1", the program will execute all statements that are indented until the indentation ends. In this example, it'll print "Hello World", followed by "How are you?".

Alternatively, if the value stored in `userInput` is "2", the program will print "Python Rocks", followed by "I love Python".

For all other values, the program will print "You did not enter a valid number".

Run the program three times, enter 1, 2 and 3 respectively for each run. You'll get the following output:

```
Enter 1 or 2: 1
Hello World
How are you?

Enter 1 or 2: 2
Python Rocks!
I love Python

Enter 1 or 2: 3
You did not enter a valid number
```

6.3 Inline If

An inline `if` statement is a simpler form of an `if` statement and is more convenient if you only need to perform a simple task.

The syntax is:

```
do Task A if condition is True else do Task B
```

For instance,

```
num1 = 12 if userInput=="1" else 13
```

This statement assigns 12 to `num1` (Task A) if `userInput` equals to "1". Else it assigns 13 to `num1` (Task B).

Another example is

```
print ("This is task A" if userInput == "1" else "This is task B")
```

This statement prints `"This is task A"` (Task A) if `userInput` equals "1". Else it prints `"This is task B"` (Task B).

6.4 For Loop

Next, let us look at the `for` loop. The `for` loop executes a block of code repeatedly until the condition in the `for` statement is no longer valid.

Looping through an iterable

In Python, an iterable refers to anything that can be looped over, such as a string, list, tuple or dictionary. The syntax for looping through an iterable is as follows:

```
for a in iterable:
    print(a)
```

Example:

```
pets = ['cats', 'dogs', 'rabbits', 'hamsters']

for myPets in pets:
    print(myPets)
```

In the program above, we first declare the list `pets` and give it the members `'cats'`, `'dogs'`, `'rabbits'` and `'hamsters'`. Next the statement `for myPets in pets:` loops through the `pets` list and assigns each member in the list to the variable `myPets`.

The first time the program runs through the `for` loop, it assigns `'cats'` to the variable `myPets`. The statement `print(myPets)` then prints the value `'cats'`. The second time the programs loops through the `for` statement, it assigns the value `'dogs'` to `myPets` and prints the value `'dogs'`. The program continues looping through the list until the end of the list is reached.

If you run the program, you'll get

```
cats
dogs
rabbits
hamsters
```

We can also display the index of the members in the list. To do that, we use the `enumerate()` function.

```
for index, myPets in enumerate(pets):
    print(index, myPets)
```

This will give us the output

```
0 cats
```

```
1 dogs
2 rabbits
3 hamster
```

To loop through a dictionary, we use the `for` loop the same way.

Example:

```
age = {'Peter': 5, 'John':7}

for i in age:
    print(i)
```

You'll get

```
Peter
John
```

as the output.

If we want to get both the dictionary key and the data, we can do it this way:

Example:

```
age = {'Peter': 5, 'John':7}

for i in age:
    print("Name = %s, Age = %d" %(i, age[i]))
```

The first time the program runs through the `for` loop, it assigns `'Peter'` to the variable `i`.
`age[i]` thus becomes `age['Peter']`, which is equal to 5.

When you run the program, you'll get

```
Name = Peter, Age = 5
Name = John, Age = 7
```

Alternatively, you can also use the `items()` method. This is a built-in method that returns each of the dictionary's key-data pair as a (key, data) tuple. Let's look at an example.

Example:

```
age = {'Peter': 5, 'John':7}

for i, j in age.items():
    print("Name = %s, Age = %d" %(i, j))
```

You'll get

```
Name = Peter, Age = 5
Name = John, Age = 7
```

The next example shows how to loop through a string.

```
message = 'Hello'

for i in message:
    print (i)
```

The output is

```
H
e
l
l
o
```

Looping through a sequence of numbers

To loop through a sequence of numbers, the built-in `range()` function comes in handy. The `range()` function generates a list of numbers and has the syntax `range(start, end, step)`.

If start is not given, the numbers generated will start from zero.

Note: A useful tip to remember here is that in Python (and most programming languages), unless otherwise stated, we always start from zero.

For instance, the index of a list and a tuple starts from zero. When using the format() method for strings, the positions of arguments start from zero.
When using the range() function, if start is not given, the numbers generated start from zero.

If step is not given, a list of consecutive numbers will be generated (i.e. step = 1). The end value must be provided. However, one weird thing about the range() function is that the given end value is never part of the generated list.

For instance,
range(5) will generate the list [0, 1, 2, 3, 4]
range(3, 10) will generate [3, 4, 5, 6, 7, 8, 9]
range(4, 10, 2) will generate [4, 6, 8]

To see how the range() function works in a for statement, try running the following code:

```
for i in range(5):
    print (i)
```

You should get
0
1
2
3
4

6.5 While Loop

The next control flow statement we are going to look at is the while loop. Like the name suggests, a while loop repeatedly executes instructions inside the loop while a certain condition remains valid. The structure of a while statement is as follows:

```
while condition is true:
    do A
```

Most of the time when using a while loop, we need to first declare a variable to function as a loop counter. Let's just call this variable counter. The condition in the while statement will evaluate the value of counter to determine if it smaller (or greater) than a certain value. If it is, the loop will be executed. Let's look at a sample program.

```
counter = 5

while counter > 0:
    print ("Counter = ", counter)
    counter = counter - 1
```

If you run the program, you'll get the following output

```
Counter = 5
Counter = 4
Counter = 3
Counter = 2
Counter = 1
```

At first look, a while statement seems to have the simplest syntax and should be the easiest to use. However, one has to be careful when using while loops due to the danger of infinite loops. Notice that in the program above, we have the line counter = counter - 1? This line is crucial. It decreases the value of `counter` by 1 and assigns this new value back to `counter`, overwriting the original value.

We need to decrease the value of `counter` by 1 so that the loop condition `while counter > 0` will eventually evaluate to `False`. If we forget to do that, the loop will keep running endlessly resulting in an infinite loop. If you want to experience this first hand, just delete the line `counter = counter - 1` and try running the program again. The program will keep printing `counter = 5` until you somehow kill the program. Not a pleasant experience especially if you have a large program and you have no idea which code segment is causing the infinite loop.

6.6 Break

When working with loops, sometimes you may want to exit the loop when a certain condition is met. To do that, we use the `break` keyword. Run the following program to see how it works.

```
j = 0
for i in range(5):
    j = j + 2
    print ('i = ', i, ', j = ', j)
    if j == 6:
        break
```

You should get the following output.

```
i =  0 , j =  2
i =  1 , j =  4
i =  2 , j =  6
```

Without the `break` keyword, the program should loop from `i = 0` to `i = 4` because we used the function `range(5)`. However with the `break` keyword, the program ends prematurely at i = 2. This is because when i = 2, j reaches the value of 6 and the break keyword causes the loop to end.

In the example above, notice that we used an if statement within a for loop. It is very common for us to 'mix-and-match' various control tools in programming, such as using a while loop inside an if statement or using a for loop inside a while loop. This is known as a nested control statement.

6.7 Continue

Another useful keyword for loops is the continue keyword. When we use continue, the rest of the loop after the keyword is skipped for that iteration. An example will make it clearer.

```
j = 0
for i in range(5):
    j = j + 2
    print ('\ni = ', i, ', j = ', j)
    if j == 6:
        continue
    print ('I will be skipped over if j=6')
```

You will get the following output:

```
i =  0 , j =  2
I will be skipped over if j=6

i =  1 , j =  4
I will be skipped over if j=6

i =  2 , j =  6

i =  3 , j =  8
I will be skipped over if j=6

i =  4 , j =  10
```

```
I will be skipped over if j=6
```

When j = 6, the line after the `continue` keyword is not printed. Other than that, everything runs as per normal.

6.8 Try, Except

The final control statement we'll look at is the `try, except` statement. This statement controls how the program proceeds when an error occurs. The syntax is as follows:

```
try:
    do something
except:
    do something else when an error occurs
```

For instance, try running the program below

```
try:
    answer = 12/0
    print (answer)
except:
    print ("An error occurred")
```

When you run the program, you'll get the message "An error occurred". This is because when the program tries to execute the statement `answer = 12/0` in the `try` block, an error occurs since you cannot divide a number by zero. The remaining of the `try` block is ignored and the statement in the `except` block is executed instead.

If you want to display more specific error messages to your users depending on the error, you can specify the error type after the `except` keyword. Try running the program below.

```
try:
    userInput1 = int(input("Please enter a
number: "))
    userInput2 = int(input("Please enter another
number: "))
    answer =userInput1/userInput2
    print ("The answer is ", answer)
    myFile = open("missing.txt", 'r')
except ValueError:
    print ("Error: You did not enter a number")
except ZeroDivisionError:
    print ("Error: Cannot divide by zero")
except Exception as e:
    print ("Unknown error: ", e)
```

The list below shows the various outputs for different user inputs. >>> denotes the user input and => denotes the output.

```
>>> Please enter a number: m
=> Error: You did not enter a number
```

Reason: User entered a string which cannot be cast into an integer. This is a ValueError. Hence, the statement in the except ValueError block is displayed.

```
>>> Please enter a number: 12
>>> Please enter another number: 0
=> Error: Cannot divide by zero
```

Reason: userInput2 = 0. Since we cannot divide a number by zero, this is a ZeroDivisionError. The statement in the except ZeroDivisionError block is displayed.

```
>>> Please enter a number: 12
>>> Please enter another number: 3
=> The answer is  4.0
=> Unknown error:  [Errno 2] No such file or
directory: 'missing.txt'
```

Reason: User enters acceptable values and the line `print` ("The answer is ", answer) executes correctly. However, the next line raises an error as *missing.txt* is not found. Since this is not a `ValueError` or a `ZeroDivisionError`, the last `except` block is executed.

`ValueError` and `ZeroDivisionError` are two of the many pre-defined error types in Python. `ValueError` is raised when a built-in operation or function receives an argument that has the right type but an inappropriate value. `ZeroDivisionError` is raised when the program tries to divide by zero.

Other common errors in Python include

IOError:
Raised when an I/O operation (such as the built-in `open()` function) fails for an I/O-related reason, e.g., "file not found".

ImportError:
Raised when an import statement fails to find the module definition

IndexError:
Raised when a sequence (e.g. string, list, tuple) index is out of range.

KeyError:
Raised when a dictionary key is not found.

NameError:
Raised when a local or global name is not found.

TypeError:
Raised when an operation or function is applied to an object of inappropriate type.

For a complete list of all the error types in Python, you can refer to https://docs.python.org/3/library/exceptions.html.

Python also comes with pre-defined error messages for each of the different types of errors. If you want to display the message, you use the `as` keyword after the error type. For instance, to display the default `ValueError` message, you write:

```
except ValueError as e:
    print (e)
```

`e` is the variable name assigned to the error. You can give it some other names, but it is common practice to use `e`. The last `except` statement in our program

```
except Exception as e:
    print ("Unknown error: ", e)
```

is an example of using the pre-defined error message. It serves as a final attempt to catch any unanticipated errors.

Chapter 7: Functions and Modules

In our previous chapters, we've briefly mentioned functions and modules. In this chapter, let's look at them in detail. To reiterate, all programming languages come with built-in codes that we can use to make our lives easier as programmers. These codes consist of pre-written classes, variables and functions for performing certain common tasks and are saved in files known as modules. Let's first look at functions.

7.1 What are Functions?

Functions are simply pre-written codes that perform a certain task. For an analogy, think of the mathematical functions available in MS Excel. To add numbers, we can use the sum() function and type sum(A1:A5) instead of typing A1+A2+A3+A4+A5.

Depending on how the function is written, whether it is part of a class (a class is a concept in object-oriented programming which we will cover in subsequent chapters) and how you import it, we can call a function simply by typing the name of the function or by using the dot notation. Some functions require us to pass data in for them to perform their tasks. These data are known as arguments and we pass them to the function by enclosing their values in parentheses ( ) separated by commas.

For instance, to use the `print()` function for displaying text on the screen, we call it by typing `print("Hello World")` where `print` is the name of the function and "`Hello World`" is the argument.

On the other hand, to use the `replace()` function for manipulating text strings, we have to type

```
newString = "Hello World".replace("World",
"Universe")
```

where `replace` is the name of the function and `"World"` and `"Universe"` are the arguments. The string before the dot (i.e. `"Hello World"`) is the string that will be affected. Hence, `"Hello World"` will be changed to `"Hello Universe"`.

Some functions may return a result after performing their tasks. In this case, the `replace()` function returns the string `"Hello Universe"`, which we then assign to `newString`. If you print `newString` using the following statement

```
print(newString)
```

you'll get

```
Hello Universe
```

7.2 Defining Your Own Functions

We can define our own functions in Python and reuse them throughout the program. The syntax for defining a function is as follows:

```
def functionName(list of parameters):
    code detailing what the function should do
    return [expression]
```

There are two keywords here, `def` and `return`.

`def` tells the program that the indented code from the next line onwards is part of the function. `return` is the keyword that we use to return an answer from the function. There can be more than one `return` statements in a function. However, once the function executes a `return` statement, the function will exit. If your function does not need to return any value, you can omit the `return` statement. Alternatively, you can write `return` or `return None`.

Let us now define our first function. Suppose we want to determine if a given number is a prime number. Here's how we can define the function using the modulus (%) operator we learned in Chapter 3.4 and the `for` loop and `if` statement we learned in Chapter 6.

```
def checkIfPrime (numberToCheck):
    for x in range(2, numberToCheck):
        if (numberToCheck%x == 0):
            return False
    return True
```

The function above has one parameter called `numberToCheck`. Parameters are variables that are used to store the arguments that we pass in to the function.

Lines 2 and 3 uses a `for` loop to divide the parameter `numberToCheck` by all numbers from 2 to `numberToCheck` − 1 to determine if the remainder is zero. If the remainder is zero, `numberToCheck` is not a prime number. Line 4 will return `False` and the function will exit.

If by last iteration of the `for` loop, none of the division gives a remainder of zero, the function will reach Line 5, and return `True`. The function will then exit.

To use this function, we type `checkIfPrime(13)` and assign it to a variable like this

```
answer = checkIfPrime(13)
```

Here we are passing in 13 as the argument, which will be stored in `numberToCheck`. The `for` loop then runs to check if `numberToCheck` is prime and returns either `True` or `False`. We can print the answer by typing `print(answer)`. We'll get the output: `True`.

7.3 Variable Scope

An important concept to understand when defining a function is the concept of variable scope. Variables defined inside a function are treated differently than variables defined outside. There are two main differences.

Firstly, any variable declared <u>inside</u> a function is only accessible within the function. These are known as local variables. Any variable declared outside a function is known as a global variable and is accessible anywhere in the program.

To understand this, try the code below:

```
message1 = "Global Variable"

def myFunction():
    print("\nINSIDE THE FUNCTION")
    #Global variables are accessible inside a
function
    print (message1)
    #Declaring a local variable
    message2 = "Local Variable"
    print (message2)

'''
Calling the function
Note that myFunction() has no parameters.
Hence, when we call this function,
we use a pair of empty parentheses.
'''
myFunction()

print("\nOUTSIDE THE FUNCTION")

#Global variables are accessible outside
function
print (message1)
```

```
#Local variables are NOT accessible outside
function.
print (message2)
```

If you run the program, you will get the output below.

```
INSIDE THE FUNCTION
Global Variable
Local Variable

OUTSIDE THE FUNCTION
Global Variable
NameError: name 'message2' is not defined
```

In the code above, `message1` is a global variable while `message2` is a local variable declared inside the function `myFunction()`. Within the function, both the local and global variables are accessible. Outside the function, the local variable `message2` is no longer accessible. We get a `NameError` when we try to access it outside the function.

The second concept to understand about variable scope is that if a local variable shares the same name as a global variable, any code inside the function is accessing the local variable. Any code outside is accessing the global variable. Try running the code below

```
message1 = "Global Variable (shares same name as
a local variable)"

def myFunction():
    message1 = "Local Variable (shares same name
as a global variable)"
    print("\nINSIDE THE FUNCTION")
    print (message1)

# Calling the function
```

```
myFunction()

# Printing message1 OUTSIDE the function
print ("\nOUTSIDE THE FUNCTION")
print (message1)
```

You'll get the output as follows:

```
INSIDE THE FUNCTION
Local Variable (shares same name as a global
variable)

OUTSIDE THE FUNCTION
Global Variable (shares same name as a local
variable)
```

When we print `message1` inside the function, it prints `"Local Variable (shares same name as a global variable)"` as it is printing the local variable. When we print it outside, it is accessing the global variable and hence prints `"Global Variable (shares same name as a local variable)"`.

7.4 Default Parameter Values

Now that we understand how functions and variable scope work, let us look at some interesting variations that Python allows when defining a function. First, let's look at default values.

Python allows us to define default values for the parameters of a function. If a parameter has a default value, we do not have to pass in any value for the parameter when calling the method. For instance, suppose a function has 5 parameters a, b, c, d and e. We can define the function as

```
def someFunction(a, b, c=1, d=2, e=3):
    print(a, b, c, d, e)
```

Here, we assign default values for the last three parameters. All parameters with default values must be placed at the end of the parameter list. In other words, we <u>cannot</u> define a function as follows because r comes after q which has a default value:

```
def someIncorrectFunction(p, q=1, r):
    print(p, q, r)
```

To call someFunction(), we can write

```
someFunction(10, 20)
```

we'll get

```
10, 20, 1, 2, 3
```

We do not have to pass in any values for c, d and e.

If we write

```
someFunction(10, 20, 30, 40)
```

we'll get

```
10, 20, 30, 40, 3
```

The two additional arguments that we pass in (30 and 40) are assigned to the parameters with default values in order. Hence, 30 replaces the default value for c while 40 replaces d.

7.5 Variable Length Argument List

In addition to having default values for parameters, Python also allows us to pass a variable number of arguments to a function. This is very useful if we do not know the number of arguments a function has in advance. For instance, we may have a function that adds a series of numbers, but we do not know how many numbers there are in advance. In cases like this, we can use the * symbol. The example below shows how this can be done.

```
def addNumbers(*num):
    sum = 0
    for i in num:
        sum = sum + i
    print(sum)
```

When we add a single asterisk in front of num, we are telling the compiler that num stores a variable-length argument list that contains several items.

The function then loops through the argument to find the sum of all the numbers and return the answer.

To call the function, we write

```
addNumbers(1, 2, 3, 4, 5)
```

we'll get 15 as the output. We can also add more numbers by writing

```
addNumbers(1, 2, 3, 4, 5, 6, 7, 8)
```

we'll get 36 as the output.

As we can see in the examples above, when we add an asterisk in front of a parameter name, we can pass in a variable number of arguments to the function. This is known as a **non-keyworded** variable length argument list.

If we want to pass in a **keyworded** variable length argument list to the function, we can use double asterisks.

For instance, consider the following example:

```
def printMemberAge(**age):
    for i, j in age.items():
        print("Name = %s, Age = %s" %(i, j))
```

This function has a parameter called `age`. The double asterisks denote that this parameter stores a keyworded variable length argument list, which is essentially a dictionary. The `for` loop then loops through the argument and prints out the values. To call the function, we can write

```
printMemberAge(Peter = 5, John = 7)
```

we'll get

```
Name = Peter, Age = 5
Name = John, Age = 7
```

If we write

```
printMemberAge(Peter = 5, John = 7, Yvonne = 10)
```

we'll get

```
Name = Peter, Age = 5
Name = John, Age = 7
Name = Yvonne, Age = 10
```

If our function uses a normal argument (also known as a formal argument), a non-keyworded variable length argument list and a keyworded variable length argument list, we must define the function using the following order:

```
def someFunction2(farg, *args, **kwargs):
```

That is, the formal argument must come first, followed by the non-keyworded argument and the keyworded argument in that order.

7.6 Importing Modules

Python comes with a large number of built-in functions. These functions are saved in files known as modules. To use the built-in codes in Python modules, we have to import them into our programs first. We do that by using the `import` keyword. There are three ways to do it.

The first way is to import the entire module by writing `import moduleName`.

For instance, to import the buit-in `random` module that comes with Python, we write `import random`.
To use the `randrange()` function in the `random` module, we write
`random.randrange(1, 10)`.

If you find it too troublesome to write `random` each time you use the function, you can import the module by writing `import random as r` (where `r` is any name of your choice). Now to use the `randrange()` function, you simply write
`r.randrange(1, 10)`.

The third way to import modules is to import specific functions from the module by writing
`from moduleName import name1[, name2[, ... nameN]]`.

For instance, to import the `randrange()` function from the `random` module, we write `from random import randrange`. If we want to import more than one functions, we separate them with a comma. To import the `randrange()` and `randint()` functions, we write `from random import randrange, randint`. To use the function now, we do not have to use the dot notation anymore. Just write `randrange(1, 10)`.

7.7 Creating our Own Module

Besides importing built-in modules, we can also create our own modules. This is very useful if you have some functions that you want to reuse in other programming projects in future.

Creating a module is simple. Simply save the file with a .py extension and put it in the same folder as the Python file that you are going to import it from.

Suppose you want to use the `checkIfPrime()` function defined earlier in another Python script. Here's how you do it. First save the code above as *prime.py* on your desktop. *prime.py* should have the following code.

```
def checkIfPrime (numberToCheck):
    for x in range(2, numberToCheck):
        if (numberToCheck%x == 0):
            return False
    return True
```

Next, create another Python file and name it *usecheckifprime.py*. Save it on your desktop as well. *usecheckifprime.py* should have the following code.

```
import prime
answer = prime.checkIfPrime(13)
print (answer)
```

Now run *usecheckifprime.py*. You should get the output `True`. Simple as that.

However, suppose you want to store *prime.py* and *usecheckifprime.py* in different folders. You are going to have to add some codes to *usecheckifprime.py* to tell the Python interpreter where to find the module.

Say you created a folder named 'MyPythonModules' in your C drive to store *prime.py*. You need to add the following code to the top of your *usecheckifprime.py* file (<u>before</u> the line `import prime`).

```
import sys

if 'C:\\MyPythonModules' not in sys.path:
    sys.path.append('C:\\MyPythonModules')
```

`sys.path` refers to your Python's system path. This is the list of directories that Python goes through to search for modules and files. The code above appends the folder 'C:\MyPythonModules' to your system path.

Now you can put *prime.py* in C:\MyPythonModules and *usecheckifprime.py* in any other folder of your choice.

Chapter 8: Working with Files

Cool! We've come to Chapter 8. In this chapter, we'll look at how to work with external files.

In Chapter 5 previously, we learned how to get input from users using the `input()` function. However, in some cases, getting users to enter data into our program may not be practical, especially if our program needs to work with large amounts of data. In cases like this, a more convenient way is to prepare the needed information as an external file and get our programs to read the information from the file. In this chapter, we are going to learn to do that. Ready?

8.1 Opening and Reading Text Files

The first type of file we are going to read from is a simple text file with multiple lines of text. To do that, let's first create a text file with the following lines.

Learn Python in One Day and Learn It Well
Python for Beginners with Hands-on Project
The only book you need to start coding in Python immediately
http://www.learncodingfast.com/python

Save this text file as *myfile.txt* to your desktop. Next, fire up IDLE and create a new file. Type the code below and save the file as *fileoperation.py* to your desktop too.

```
f = open ('myfile.txt', 'r')

firstline = f.readline()
secondline = f.readline()
print (firstline)
print (secondline)

f.close()
```

The first line in the code opens the file. Before we can read from any file, we have to open it (just like you need to open an ebook on your kindle device or app to read it). The `open()` function does that and requires two arguments:

The first argument is the path to the file. If you did not save *fileoperation.py* and *myfile.txt* in the same folder (desktop in this case), you need to replace `'myfile.txt'` with the actual path where you stored the text file. For instance, if you stored it in a folder named 'PythonFiles' on your C drive, you have to write `'C:\\PythonFiles\\myfile.txt'` (with double backslash \\).

The second argument is the mode. This specifies how the file will be used. The commonly used modes are

'r' mode:
For reading only.

'w' mode:
For writing only.
If the specified file does not exist, it will be created.
If the specified file exists, any existing data on the file will be erased.

'a' mode:
For appending.
If the specified file does not exist, it will be created.
If the specified file exist, any data written to the file is automatically added to the end

'r+' mode:
For both reading and writing.

After opening the file, the next statement `firstline = f.readline()` reads the first line in the file and assigns it to the variable `firstline`.

Each time the `readline()` function is called, it reads a new line from the file. In our program, `readline()` was called twice. Hence the first two lines will be read. When you run the program, you'll get the output:

Learn Python in One Day and Learn It Well

Python for Beginners with Hands-on Project

You'll notice that a line break is inserted after each line. This is because the `readline()` function adds the '\n' characters to the end of each line. If you do not want the extra line between each line of text, you can do `print(firstline, end = '')`. This will remove the '\n' characters. Note that '' is made up of two single quotes, not a single double quote.

After reading and printing the first two lines, the last sentence `f.close()` closes the file. You should always close the file once you finish reading it to free up any system resources.

8.2 Using a For Loop to Read Text Files

In addition to using the `readline()` method above to read a text file, we can also use a `for` loop. In fact, the `for` loop is a more elegant and efficient way to read text files. The following program shows how this is done.

```
f = open ('myfile.txt', 'r')

for line in f:
    print (line, end = '')

f.close()
```

The `for` loop loops through the text file line by line. When you run it, you'll get

Learn Python in One Day and Learn It Well
Python for Beginners with Hands-on Project
The only book you need to start coding in Python immediately
http://www.learncodingfast.com/python

8.3 Writing to a Text File

Now that we've learned how to open and read a file, let's try writing to it. To do that, we'll use the 'a' (append) mode. You can also use the 'w' mode, but you'll erase all previous content in the file if the file already exists. Try running the following program.

```
f = open ('myfile.txt', 'a')

f.write('\nThis sentence will be appended.')
f.write('\nPython is Fun!')

f.close()
```

Here we use the write() function to append the two sentences 'This sentence will be appended.' and 'Python is Fun!' to the file, each starting on a new line since we used the escape characters '\n'. You'll get

Learn Python in One Day and Learn It Well
Python for Beginners with Hands-on Project
The only book you need to start coding in Python immediately
http://www.learncodingfast.com/python
This sentence will be appended.
Python is Fun!

8.4 Opening and Reading Text Files by Buffer Size

Sometimes, we may want to read a file by buffer size so that our program does not use too much memory resources. To do that, we can use the `read()` function (instead of the `readline()` function) which allows us to specify the buffer size we want. Try the following program:

```
inputFile = open ('myfile.txt', 'r')
outputFile = open ('myoutputfile.txt', 'w')

msg = inputFile.read(10)

while len(msg):
    outputFile.write(msg)
    msg = inputFile.read(10)

inputFile.close()
outputFile.close()
```

First, we open two files, the *inputFile.txt* and *outputFile.txt* files for reading and writing respectively.

Next, we use the statement `msg = inputFile.read(10)` and a `while` loop to loop through the file 10 bytes at a time. The value 10 in the parentheses tells the `read()` function to only read 10 bytes. The `while` condition `while len(msg):` checks the length of the variable `msg`. As long as the length is not zero, the loop will run.

Within the `while` loop, the statement `outputFile.write(msg)` writes the message to the output file. After writing the message, the statement `msg = inputFile.read(10)` reads the next 10 bytes and keeps doing it until the entire file is read. When that happens, the program closes both files.

When you run the program, a new file *myoutputfile.txt* will be created. When you open the file, you'll notice that it has the same content as your input file *myfile.txt*. To prove that only 10 bytes is read at a time, you can change the line

`outputFile.write(msg)` in the program to
`outputFile.write(msg + '\n')`. Now run the program
again. *myoutputfile.txt* now contains lines with at most 10
characters. Here's a segment of what you'll get.

Learn Pyth
on in One
Day and Le
arn It Wel

8.5 Opening, Reading and Writing Binary Files

Binary files refer to any file that contains non-text, such as image
or video files. To work with binary files, we simply use the `'rb'`
or `'wb'` mode. Copy a jpeg file onto your desktop and rename it
myimage.jpg. Now edit the program above by changing the first
two line lines

```
inputFile = open ('myfile.txt', 'r')
outputFile = open ('myoutputfile.txt', 'w')
```

to

```
inputFile = open ('myimage.jpg', 'rb')
outputFile = open ('myoutputimage.jpg', 'wb')
```

Make sure you also change the statement
`outputFile.write(msg + '\n')` back to
`outputFile.write(msg)`.

Run the new program. You should have an additional image file
named *myoutputimage.jpg* on your desktop. When you open the
image file, it should look exactly like *myimage.jpg*.

8.6 Deleting and Renaming Files

Two other useful functions we need to learn when working with files are the `remove()` and `rename()` functions. These functions are available in the `os` module and have to be imported before we can use them.

The `remove()` function deletes a file. The syntax is `remove(filename)`. For instance, to delete *myfile.txt*, we write `remove('myfile.txt')`.

The `rename()` function renames a file. The syntax is `rename(old name, new name)`. To rename *oldfile.txt* to *newfile.txt*, we write `rename('oldfile.txt', 'newfile.txt')`.

Chapter 9: Object Oriented Programming Part 1

We have covered a fair bit so far. In the next two chapters, we are going to look at another important concept in Python programming – the concept of object-oriented programming.

In this chapter, we'll learn what object-oriented programming is and how we can write our own classes and create objects from them. In the next chapter, we'll discuss inheritance and cover some other advanced topics in object-oriented programming.

Let's get started!

9.1 What is Object-Oriented Programming?

Simply stated, object-oriented programming is an approach to programming that breaks a programming problem into objects that interact with each other.

Objects are created from templates known as classes. You can think of a class as the blueprint of a building. An object is the actual "building" that we build based on the blueprint.

To understand how object-oriented programming works, let's start by coding a simple class together.

9.2 Writing our own class

To write our own class, we use the `class` keyword followed by the name of the class.

For instance, to create a `Staff` class, we write

```
class Staff:
    #contents of the class
```

It is common practice to use PascalCasing when naming our classes. PascalCasing refers to the practice of capitalizing the first letter of each word, including the first word (e.g. ThisIsAClassName). This is the convention that we'll be following in the book.

A class consists of variables and functions. As we learned in previous chapters, variables are for storing data while functions are code blocks that perform certain tasks for us. If a function exists within a class, it is more commonly referred to as a method.

You can think of a class as a template for grouping related data and methods together.

For instance, supposed we have a class called Staff. This class can be used to store all the relevant information about a staff in the company. Within the class, we can declare two variables to store the name and position of the staff. In addition, we can also code a method called calculatePay() to calculate the pay of the staff.

Let's look at how to do that.

Fire up IDLE and create a new file called *classdemo.py*. Add the following code to *classdemo.py*.

```python
class Staff:
    def __init__ (self, pPosition, pName, pPay):
        self.position = pPosition
        self.name = pName
        self.pay = pPay
        print ('Creating Staff object')

    def __str__ (self):
        return "Position = %s, Name = %s, Pay = %d" % (self.position, self.name, self.pay)
```

```
def calculatePay(self):
    prompt = '\nEnter number of hours worked
for %s: ' %(self.name)
    hours = input(prompt)
    prompt = 'Enter the hourly rate for %s:
' %(self.name)
    hourlyRate = input(prompt)
    self.pay = int(hours)*int(hourlyRate)
    return self.pay
```

In the code above, we first define a class called `Staff` by writing

```
class Staff:
```

Next, we define a special method called __init__ for the class. This is known as the initializer of the class. It is always named init with **two** underscores in front and at the back. Python comes with a large number of special methods. All special methods have two underscores in front and at the back of their names. We'll discuss special methods in Chapter 10.4 later.

An initializer is called whenever an object of the class is created. Do not worry if you don't know what this means. We'll learn how to create an object of the class later.

For now, all that you have to know is an initializer is frequently used to initialize the variables (i.e. give them initial values) in the class.

In our class, we have three variables – `position`, `name` and `pay`. These variables are known as instance variables, in contrast to local variables (covered in Chapter 7.3) and class variables (to be covered later in Chapter 9.6). Instance variables are variables that are prefixed with a `self` keyword.

The `self` keyword is hard to explain at this stage. Simply stated, `self` refers to an instance itself. This statement probably sounds abstract to you. We'll explore the meaning of `self` in a later section. For now, just know that when we want to refer to instance variables in the class, we need to add `self` in front of the variable names. In addition, most methods in a class have `self` as the first parameter.

The three statements below assign three parameters of the `__init__` method (`pPosition`, `pName` and `pPay`) to the instance variables to initialize them.

```
self.position = pPosition
self.name = pName
self.pay = pPay
```

After initializing the three instance variables, we print out a simple statement `'Creating Staff object'`. That's all that the initializer does.

Writing an initializer is optional if you do not wish to initialize the instance variables when you create the object. You can always initialize them later.

Let's move on to the next method - `__str__`.

`__str__` is another special method that is commonly included when we code a class. We use it to return a human readable string that represents the class. In our example, we simply return a string that gives the values of the three instance variables. We'll look at how we use this method later.

Now, let's move on to the `calculatePay()` method.

`calcuatePay()` is a method that is used to calculate the pay of a staff. You'll notice that it is very similar to a function, except for the parameter `self`. Indeed, a method is almost identical to a function except that a method exists inside a class and most methods have `self` as a parameter.

Within the `calcuatePay()` method, we first prompt the user to enter the number of hours worked for the staff. Next, we prompt for the hourly rate and calculate the pay based on these two values. We then assign the result to the instance variable `self.pay` and return the value of `self.pay`.

You may notice that in this method, we do not add `self` in front of some variables (such as `prompt`, `hours` and `hourlyRate`). This is because these variables are local variables and only exist within the `calculatePay()` method. We do not need to add `self` in front of local variables.

That's all there is to the class that we wrote. To recap, our class has the following components

Instance Variables

```
position
name
pay
```

Methods

```
__init__
__str__
calculatePay()
```

9.3 Instantiating an Object

Next, let's learn how to use this class.

In order to use the class, we have to create an object from it. This is known as instantiating an object. An object is also known as an instance. Although there are some differences between an object and an instance, these are more semantic differences and the two words are frequently used interchangeably.

Let's instantiate a `Staff` object now. We will do that in the Python Shell. Before we can use the `Staff` class, we need to first run it. Select Run > Run Module from the *classdemo.py* file to run it. This will open the Python Shell.

Now we are ready to instantiate a `Staff` object.

To do that, we write

```
officeStaff1 = Staff('Basic', 'Yvonne', 0)
```

This is a bit similar to how we declare a variable where we write

```
userAge = 10
```

In this case, `officeStaff1` is the variable name. However, since `officeStaff1` is not an integer, we do not assign a number to it. Instead, we write `Staff('Basic', 'Yvonne', 0)` on the right hand side. When we do that, we are essentially asking the `Staff` class to create a `Staff` object and to use the `__init__` method to initialize the instance variables in the class.

Notice that we have three values `'Basic'`, `'Yvonne'` and `0` inside the parentheses? These are for the parameters `pPosition`, `pName` and `pPay` in the `__init__` method that we coded earlier. We use these three values to initialize the instance variables `position`, `name` and `pay` respectively. You might be wondering what happened to the first parameter `self`? We do not need to pass in anything for the parameter `self`. It is a special parameter and Python will add it for you automatically when calling the method.

After we create that object, we assign it to `officeStaff1`.

Try typing the following statement into Shell and press enter.

```
officeStaff1 = Staff('Basic', 'Yvonne', 0)
```

You'll see the message

```
Creating Staff object
```

displayed on the screen. This indicates that the initializer is being called.

Now that we have created an object of the `Staff` class, we can use it to access the instance variables and methods inside the class. To do that, we use the dot operator after the object's name to access any instance variable or method in the `Staff` class.

For instance, to access the instance variable `name`, we type

```
officeStaff1.name
```

As we are accessing the variable using Python Shell, we do not need to use the `print()` function to display the value. However, if we are not using the Python Shell, we'll have to use the `print()` function. We'll see an example of that later in Chapter 9.6.

Try adding the following lines to Shell to see what happens.

To access the variable `name`

```
officeStaff1.name
```

Output:
```
'Yvonne'
```

To **access** the variable `position`

```
officeStaff1.position
```

Output:
```
'Basic'
```

To **change** variable `position` and print it again

```
#change variable position
officeStaff1.position = 'Manager'

#print position again
officeStaff1.position
```

Output:
```
'Manager'
```

To access the variable `pay`

```
officeStaff1.pay
```

Output:
```
0
```

To use `calculatePay()` method to calculate pay

```
officeStaff1.calculatePay()
```

Output:
```
Enter number of hours worked for Yvonne: 10
Enter the hourly rate for Yvonne: 15
```

To print variable `pay` again

```
officeStaff1.pay
```

Output:
```
150
```

To print a string representation of `officeStaff1`

```
print(officeStaff1)
```

Output:
```
Position = Manager, Name = Yvonne, Pay = 150
```

To print a string representation of the object, we pass in the object's name to the built-in `print()` function. When we do this, Python will call the `__str__` method that we coded earlier. In our example, we coded it to return the `position`, `name` and `pay` of `officeStaff1`.

9.4 Properties

Now that we have a basic understanding of classes and objects, let us move on to discuss properties.

In the examples above, we notice that we can access an object's instance variables using the dot operator. This makes it easy for us to read the variables and modify them when necessary. However, this flexibility also poses some problems. For instance, we may accidentally change the position of `officeStaff1` to a non-existent position. Or we may change the pay of `officeStaff1` to an incorrect amount.

To prevent such errors from occurring, we can use properties. Properties provide us with a way to check the values of the changes that we want to make before allowing the change to occur.

To demonstrate how properties work, we'll add one for the variable `position`. Specifically, we'll add a property to ensure that the variable `position` can only be set to either `'Basic'` or `'Manager'`.

However, before we do that, we want to first change the name of the instance variable from `position` to `_position`. Adding a single underscore in front of a variable name is a customary way to signal to other programmers that they should not touch this variable directly.

In Python programming, there is a commonly used phrase that says "we're all consenting adults here". We are all expected to behave like an adult. Adding a single underscore in front of a variable tells other programmers that you're trusting them to behave responsibly and not access that variable directly unless they have a compelling reason to. However technically, there is nothing stopping them from accessing the variable. If they so desire, they can still access it by writing

```
officeStaff1._position
```

Having said that, let's just make the following changes to the *classdemo.py* file to let other 'consenting adults' know they should not access `position` directly:

Change the line

```
self.position = pPosition
```

in `__init__` to

```
self._position = pPosition
```

and the line

```
return "Position = %s, Name = %s, Pay
= %d" %(self.position, self.name, self.pay)
```

in __str__ to

```
return "Position = %s, Name = %s, Pay
= %d" %(self._position, self.name, self.pay)
```

Next, let's look at how to add a property for the _position variable:

Add the following lines to the Staff class in *classdemo.py*.

```
@property
def position(self):
    print("Getter Method")
    return self._position

@position.setter
def position(self, value):
    if value == 'Manager' or value == 'Basic':
        self._position = value
    else:
        print('Position is invalid. No changes
made.')
```

Remember to indent the lines above when adding them to the Staff class. If you do not indent them, they do not belong to the Staff class.

The first line above (@property) is known as a decorator. We won't go into details about what a decorator is, but simply put, it allows us to alter the functionality of the method that follows. In this case, it changes the first position() method to a property.

This means that it is telling the compiler that whenever users type

```
officeStaff1.position
```

it should use the `position()` method that follows to get the value.

This method simply prints the message "Getter Method" and returns the value of the variable `_position`. Due to the `@property` decorator that changes the method to a property, we do not have to type `officeStaff1.position()` to access the method. We access it like a variable without the parentheses.

Next, we have another decorator `@position.setter` followed by a second `position()` method.

This decorator tells the compiler that when users try to update the value of `_position` by writing something like

```
officeStaff1.position = 'Manager'
```

it should use the `position()` method that follows to update the value.

This second `position()` method is known as a setter method. It has a parameter called `value` that is assigned to `_position` as long as `value` is either `'Manager'` or `'Basic'`. If `value` is neither of these, the message `'Position is invalid. No changes made.'` is displayed.

Now, save the file and run it again.

Type the following statement into Shell:

```
officeStaff1 = Staff('Basic', 'Yvonne', 0)
```

To access the position of `officeStaff1`, we write

```
officeStaff1.position
```

We'll get

```
Getter Method
'Basic'
```

as the output.

Previously when we typed

```
officeStaff1.position
```

we were accessing the variable `position` directly. Now when we type

```
officeStaff1.position
```

we are no longer accessing the variable. Instead, we are accessing the getter method of the `position` property. This is illustrated by the fact that we get an extra line (`Getter Method`) as the output.

It is not a coincidence that we name the property `position`, which is the original name of the variable before we changed it to `_position`.

When we do it this way, users can access the position of the staff the same way that they were used to, by writing `officeStaff1.position`. Even though we made a number of changes to *classdemo.py* in the back end, end users are not affected by these changes (unless they try to change the position of the staff to an invalid value).

Now, let's try to change the position of `officeStaff1`. Type the following into Shell

```
officeStaff1.position = 'Manager'
```

This changes the position of the staff to 'Manager'.

Verify that by typing

```
officeStaff1.position
```

You'll get

```
Getter Method
'Manager'
```

as the output.

Next, let's try to change the position to 'CEO'. Type the following into Shell

```
officeStaff1.position = 'CEO'
```

You'll get

```
Position is invalid. No changes made.
```

as the output.

This demonstrates that the setter method has prevented us from changing the position of a staff to an invalid value. You can verify that position is not changed by typing

```
officeStaff1.position
```

again. You'll get

```
Getter Method
'Manager'
```

as the output.

9.5 Name Mangling

Next, let's move on to discuss the concept of name mangling in Python.

In the previous section, we mentioned that if we do not want other programmers to access a certain variable directly, we indicate that by adding a single underscore in front. We then code properties to control their access. However, even if we do so, other programmers can still access that variable if they want to. In the previous example, they can simply type

```
officeStaff1._position
```

In Python, there is no way to really hide a variable and prevent other users from accessing it. However, if you really want to *send a strong signal* to other programmers that a certain variable should not be modified, you can add double underscores to the front of the variable name.

For instance, try typing the following code into the Python shell:

```
class A:
    def __init__(self):
        self.__x = 5
        self._y = 6
```

The code above defines a class called A. This class has two variables __x (with double underscores) and _y (with single underscore)

Next, press enter twice and key in the line below to instantiate a class A object.

```
varA = A()
```

Now, we shall try to access the two variables. If you type

```
varA._y
```

you'll get

6

as the output. However, if you type

```
varA.__x
```

you'll get an error.

Why is that so? This is because when you add double underscores in front, Python does what is known as name mangling. Essentially, when the Python compiler encounters a variable with two leading underscores, it transforms the name by adding a single underscore and the class name in front of the variable name. In other words, when it sees __x, it changes the name to _A__x.

This means that when we add a double underscore in front of a variable name, other programmers cannot access the variable by simply typing the variable name (__x in this case). This makes it harder for them to access the variable. However, if they so desire, they can still access it by typing

```
varA._A__x
```

They'll get 5 as the output.

In other words, there is no way to absolutely restrict access to a variable in Python. You can use underscores to make it more difficult to access, but a determined programmer can still access it. As we mentioned earlier, in Python, we are all consenting adults. Hence, we are expected to behave responsibly and not modify variables that we are told not to.

9.6 What is self

Now that we have an understanding of how classes work, let's explore the meaning of `self`.

In order to explain `self`, we have to first discuss the concept of class vs instance variables.

A class variable belongs to the class and is shared by all instances of that class. It is defined outside any method in the class.

An instance variable, on the other hand, is defined inside a method and belongs to an instance. It is always prefixed with the `self` keyword.

Let's consider an example. Supposed Peter and John both work for a company called ProgrammingLab. We can create a class called `ProgStaff` to store this information. Create a new file called *selfdemo.py* and add the following code to it:

```
class ProgStaff:
    companyName = 'ProgrammingLab'

    def __init__(self, pSalary):
        self.salary = pSalary

    def printInfo(self):
        print("Company name is",
ProgStaff.companyName)
        print("Salary is", self.salary)

peter = ProgStaff(2500)
john = ProgStaff(2500)
```

The first few lines of the code above defines a class called `ProgStaff`.

This class has a variable called `companyName` that is not defined inside any method.

Next, it has an __init__ method. Inside the __init__ method, it has a variable called `salary`. This variable is prefixed with the `self` keyword.

Finally, it also has a method called `printInfo()` that has `self` as a parameter. This method simply prints the value of `companyName` and `salary`.

After defining the class, we created two instances of the `ProgStaff` class called `peter` and `john`. We do not indent these two instantiation statements as they are not part of the `Staff` class.

Now, let's explore the difference between a class and instance variable.

Currently, the name of the company is 'ProgrammingLab'. Suppose the name is subsequently changed to 'ProgrammingSchool', we update it as follows:

```
ProgStaff.companyName = 'ProgrammingSchool'
```

Notice that we prefix the variable `companyName` with `ProgStaff`. This change affects all instances of the `ProgStaff` class (`peter` and `john` in this case).

Add the following lines to *selfdemo.py* to verify that.

```
ProgStaff.companyName = 'ProgrammingSchool'
print(peter.companyName)
print(john.companyName)
```

Notice that in the code above, as we are not typing directly into the Python Shell, we have to use the `print()` function to display the value of `companyName` for `peter` and `john`.

Save the file and run the program. You'll get the following output:

```
ProgrammingSchool
ProgrammingSchool
```

Next, suppose the salary of `peter` is increased to 2700. We update it as follows:

```
peter.salary = 2700
```

This change only affects the instance 'peter'. We can verify it by printing the salary of `peter` and `john`. Add the following lines to *selfdemo.py* and run the program:

```
peter.salary = 2700
print(peter.salary)
print(john. salary)
```

You'll get

```
2700
2500
```

as the output. Only the salary of `peter` is updated.

In summary, the main differences between a class and instance variable are:

Class Variable
1. A class variable is defined outside any method in the class
2. It can be accessed outside the class using the class name
3. Changing it affects all instances of the class

Instance Variable
1. An instance variable is defined inside a method in the class and prefixed with the `self` keyword.
2. It can be accessed outside the class using the name of the instance.
3. Changing it only affects the specific instance

In our example, `companyName` is a class variable while `salary` is an instance variable.

Now that we understand what class and instance variables are, let us move on to discuss the `printInfo()` method in the `ProgStaff` class.

This method is known as an instance method. An instance method is a method that has `self` as one of its parameters. If the method has more than one parameter, `self` must be the first parameter.

Inside the method, we use the class name to access the class variable `companyName`. In contrast, we use the `self` keyword to access the instance variable `salary`.

`self` essentially represents an instance of the class. As different instances have different names and we do not know those names yet (as we have not created them yet), we use the `self` keyword to represent them inside the class.

To call the `printInfo()` method, we type

```
john.printInfo()
```

When we call the instance method this way, Python passes in `john` to the `self` parameter implicitly for us. We do not have to do it ourselves.

Alternatively, if we prefer, we can also use the class name to call the instance method. When we do it this way, we have to pass in the instance john ourselves as shown below:

```
ProgStaff.printInfo(john)
```

Both methods give us the same output. Try adding the two statements above to *selfdemo.py* and run the program. You'll get

```
Company name is ProgrammingSchool
Salary is 2500
Company name is ProgrammingSchool
Salary is 2500
```

as the output.

9.7 Class and Static Methods

Now that we understand what self means, let us move on to discuss class and static methods.

In the previous section, we mentioned that an instance method is a method that has self as a parameter. This is the most common type of method and is the only type of method that we've been using so far.

In addition to instance methods, Python also has class and static methods. These types of methods are rarely used. Hence, we'll only do a brief discussion of them here. To start, let's create a file called *methoddemo.py*. Add the following code to the file.

```
class MethodDemo:

    a = 1

    @classmethod
    def classM(cls):
        print("Class Method. cls.a = ", cls.a)
```

```
@staticmethod
def staticM():
    print("Static method")
```

This class has a class variable `a` and two methods – `classM()` and `staticM()`.

The first method, `classM()`, is a class method.

To define a class method, we need to use the `@classmethod` decorator to inform Python that what follows is a class method.

A class method is a method that has a class object (instead of `self`) as the first parameter. `cls` is commonly used to represent that class object.

`cls` is sort of similar to `self`. The main difference is `self` refers to an instance while `cls` refers to a class. As `cls` refers to the class itself, we can use it to access our class variables. In our example, we used it to access the class variable `a`.

To call a class method, we can either use the class name or the instance name. In both cases, Python automatically passes in the class as the first argument to the method.

For instance, to call `classM()` in the example above, we can write

```
MethodDemo.classM()
```

Alternatively, we can instantiate a `MethodDemo` object and use it to call the method as shown below:

```
md1 = MethodDemo()
md1.classM()
```

Add the three statements above to *methoddemo.py* and run the program. You'll get

```
Class Method. cls.a =   1
Class Method. cls.a =   1
```

as the output.

Besides instance and class methods, Python also has static methods. A static method is a method that is not passed an instance or a class. It does not have `self` or `cls` as the first parameter. To define a static method, we use the `@staticmethod` decorator. To call a static method, we can either use the class name or the instance name. For instance, to call `staticM()` in the example above, we can write

```
md1.staticM()
```

or

```
MethodDemo.staticM()
```

We'll get

```
Static method
```

in both cases.

Class and static methods are not very commonly used. In most cases, instance methods are all that is required in a Python class.

9.8 Importing a class

We've covered quite a few object-oriented concepts in this chapter. Before we end this chapter, let us learn how to import a class into an application.

Like what we learned in Chapter 7 regarding modules, a class can also be created as a separate file and imported into an application. To do that, we need to save the class as a separate file with the .py extension. We then import it using the file name.

For instance, suppose we have the following code in a file called *myclass.py*.

```
class SomeClass:
    def __init__(self):
        print('This is SomeClass')
    def someMethod(self, a):
        print('The value of a is', a)
        self.b = 5

class SomeOtherClass:
    def __init__(self):
        print('This is SomeOtherClass')
```

This file consists of two classes: SomeClass and SomeOtherClass. We can create another .py file and import these two classes using the file name (*myclass*). We can then use this file name to access the classes inside the file.

Let's create another file and name it *importdemo.py*. Add the following code to the file and run it.

```
import myclass

sc = myclass.SomeClass()
sc.someMethod(100)

soc = myclass.SomeOtherClass()
```

You'll get

```
This is SomeClass
```

```
The value of a is 100
This is SomeOtherClass
```

as the output.

In the code above, we instantiated the objects by prefixing the class name with the file name, such as `myclass.SomeClass()` so that the compiler knows that `SomeClass` is in the file *myclass.py*.

Alternatively, you can choose to import using the statement below:

```
from myclass import SomeClass, SomeOtherClass
```

If you do it this way, you do not need to prefix the file name when instantiating an object. For instance, to instantiate a `SomeClass` object, you simply write

```
sc = SomeClass()
```

Chapter 10: Object Oriented Programming Part 2

Now, let us move on to some of the more advanced topics in object-oriented programming. In this chapter, we'll learn about inheritance, polymorphism and overloading operators.

10.1 Inheritance

Inheritance is one of the key concepts of object-oriented programming. Simply stated, inheritance allows us to create a new class from an existing class so that we can effectively reuse existing code.

10.2 Writing the Child Class

To understand how inheritance works, let us expand on the `Staff` class that we wrote earlier in Chapter 9. To recap, our `Staff` class has the following attributes:

Instance Variables

```
_position
name
pay
```

Methods

```
__init__
__str__
calculatePay()
```

This class served us well in Chapter 9 when we used it to calculate the pay of a basic staff who is paid on an hourly basis.

However, suppose in addition to having basic staff, the company also has a manager who has a slightly different pay scheme. For instance, suppose the company has a manager who earns an allowance on top of a basic hourly pay, how can we modify the class to accommodate this?

The best way to do this is to create a sub class. A sub class is also known as a derived class or a child class. The class from which it is derived is known as a base class, a super class or a parent class.

The main feature of a sub class is that it inherits all the variables and methods from the parent class. In other words, it can use those variables and methods as if they are part of its own code without having to code them again. In addition, a sub class can have additional variables and methods that do not exist in the parent class. Let's look at how this can be done.

We shall create a sub class called `ManagementStaff`. Add the following line to *classdemo.py*:

```
class ManagementStaff(Staff):
```

Here, we are creating a new class called `ManagementStaff`. We indicate that `ManagementStaff` is a subclass of `Staff` by adding the word `Staff` in parentheses after the class name.

Next, we shall code the `__init__` method for the subclass.

One of the main reasons for coding subclasses is to facilitate code reuse. One way to do it is to use a built-in function called `super()`.

Let's look at how to do that. Earlier in Chapter 9, we have already coded an `__init__` method for the `Staff` class. This method initializes the three instance variables `_position`, `name` and `pay`. Now we shall make use of this method in the sub class.

Add the following method to the `ManagementStaff` class.

```
def __init__ (self, pName, pPay, pAllowance,
pBonus):
    super().__init__('Manager', pName, pPay)
    self.allowance = pAllowance
    self.bonus = pBonus
```

The `__init__` method in `ManagementStaff` has five parameters – `self, pName, pPay, pAllowance` and `pBonus`.

Within the method, the first line uses the `super()` function to call the `__init__` method in the base class. The `super()` function is a pre-built function that we can use in a sub class to call a method in the super class.

In Python 3, when we use `super()` to call a method in the parent class, we do not have to pass in any value for the `self` parameter.

Hence, in our example, we only need to pass in three values (the string `'Manager'` and the parameters `pName` and `pPay`) to the base class `__init__` method. The base class method will be called and the string `'Manager'` will be assigned to `_position` while `pName` and `pPay` will be assigned to `name` and `pay` respectively.

If you are using Python 2, the syntax for using the `super()` method is slightly different. To use `super()` in Python 2, you need to pass in the sub class name and the keyword `self`. In other words, in our example, you need to write

```
super(ManagementStaff, self).__init__('Manager',
pName, pPay)
```

This syntax is still supported in Python 3 and some programmers choose to stick to this syntax for backwards compatibility.

Besides using the `super()` function, we can also use the parent class name to call a method in the base class. To do that, we write

```
Staff.__init__(self, 'Manager', pName, pPay)
```

All three methods above achieve the same outcome in this example. All has its pros and cons and a debate of which is better is beyond the scope of this book. In most cases, deciding on which one to use is largely a matter of preference.

After calling the `__init__` method in the base class, the sub class `__init__` method uses the two statements below to assign the parameters `pAllowance` and `pBonus` to the instance variables `allowance` and `bonus` respectively.

```
self.allowance = pAllowance
self.bonus = pBonus
```

These two instance variables only exist in the subclass. They do not exist in the super class. That's all for the `__init__` method in the sub class.

Now, let us code a method to calculate the pay of a management staff. Add the following method to `ManagementStaff`.

```
def calculatePay(self):
    basicPay = super().calculatePay()
    self.pay = basicPay + self.allowance
    return self.pay
```

Notice that this method uses the `super()` function again to call the `calculatePay()` method in the base class. After calling the base class method, we assign the result to the variable `basicPay`. `basicPay` is a local variable that only exists within the `calculatePay()` method. Hence, you do not need to prefix it with the keyword `self`.

Next, we add the value of `basicPay` to the instance variable `allowance` to calculate the total pay of the management staff. We then assign it to the instance variable `pay` and return this value in the next statement.

That concludes the `calculatePay()` method in the sub class.

Recall that we mentioned earlier that a sub class inherits all the variables and methods from its base class? This means that we do not need to code a new `calculatePay()` method for the subclass; it already exists. However, if we choose to code a new version for the subclass, this new version replaces the version that the sub class inherited. This is known as *overriding*, which is what we did in this example.

Now, let us add a new method to the subclass. Suppose a management staff is also entitled to performance bonus if his/her performance grade is an 'A'. To calculate the performance bonus of a management staff, we can add a new method to the `ManagementStaff` class:

```
def calculatePerfBonus(self):
    prompt = 'Enter performance grade for %s: ' %(self.name)
    grade = input(prompt)
    if (grade == 'A'):
        self.bonus = 1000
    else:
        self.bonus = 0
    return self.bonus
```

This method first prompts the user to enter the performance grade for the management staff. It then assigns either 1000 or 0 to the instance variable `bonus` based on the performance grade entered. Finally, it returns the value of `bonus` in the next statement.

With that, our `ManagementStaff` class is complete. The class has the following content:

Instance Variables

Inherited from `Staff`:
```
_position
name
pay
```

Declared in `ManagementStaff`:
```
allowance
bonus
```

Methods

Inherited and not overridden:
```
__str__
```

Inherited and Overridden:
```
__init__
calculatePay()
```

Declared in `ManagementStaff`:
```
calculatePerfBonus()
```

Before we end this section, we shall derive one more sub class from `Staff`. This time, the derived class is called `BasicStaff`. The code is shown below:

```
class BasicStaff(Staff):
```

```
def __init__(self, pName, pPay):
    super().__init__('Basic', pName, pPay)
```

This sub class only overrides the __init__ method in the base class. The __init__ method passes in the string 'Basic' to the base class initializer so that the instance variable _position will be assigned automatically when we instantiate a BasicStaff object. Other than that, the sub class inherits all other variables and methods from the base class. The class has the following content:

<u>Instance Variables</u>

Inherited from Staff:
```
_position
name
pay
```

<u>Methods</u>

Inherited and not overridden:
```
__str__
calculatePay()
```

Inherited and Overridden:
```
__init__
```

10.3 Instantiating a Child Object

Now that we have coded our child classes, let us create a separate .py file to make use of these classes.

Create a new file in IDLE and name it *inheritancedemo.py*. Add the following lines to the file:

```
import classdemo
```

```
peter = classdemo.BasicStaff('Peter', 0)
john = classdemo.ManagementStaff('John', 0,
1000, 0)

print(peter)
print(john)

print('Peter\'s Pay = ', peter.calculatePay())

print('John\'s Pay = ', john.calculatePay())
print('John\'s Performance Bonus = ',
john.calculatePerfBonus())
```

In the code above, we first import the three classes (`Staff`, `ManagementStaff` and `BasicStaff`) using the statement

```
import classdemo
```

Next, we instantiate two child objects – `peter` and `john` – for the two subclasses `BasicStaff` and `ManagementStaff` respectively.

For `peter`, we passed in `'Peter'` and 0 for the instance variables `name` and `pay` respectively.

For `john`, we passed in `'John'`, 0, 1000 and 0 for the instance variables `name`, `pay`, `allowance` and `bonus` respectively.

Next, we use the two objects to call the __str__ method.

Although we did not code the __str__ method in the two subclasses, we can still use this method as both subclasses have inherited the method from the base class. This facilitates code reuse as we do not need to rewrite the __str__ method for both the child classes.

After calling the __str__ method, we call the `caculatePay()` method for `peter` and `john` and display the information on the screen. Finally, we call the `calculatePerfBonus()` method for `john`. If we run the program and enter the relevant information when prompted, we'll get the following output:

```
Creating Staff object
Creating Staff object
Position = Basic, Name = Peter, Pay = 0
Position = Manager, Name = John, Pay = 0
Enter number of hours worked for Peter: 120
Enter the hourly rate for Peter: 15
Peter's Pay =  1800

Enter number of hours worked for John: 150
Enter the hourly rate for John: 20
John's Pay =  4000
Enter performance grade for John: A
John's Performance Bonus =  1000
```

As `peter` uses the `calculatePay()` method inherited from the base class, the pay for `peter` is 1800 (i.e. 120*15). In contrast, the pay for `john` is 4000 as it uses the `calculatePay()` method in the `ManagementStaff` subclass. The `calculatePay()` method in the `ManagementStaff` subclass overrides the method in the base class. Hence, the pay is 150*20 + 1000 (i.e. an allowance of 1000 is added).

After we calculate the pay for `peter` and `john`, we calculate the performance bonus for `john`. As his performance grade is 'A', he is awarded a bonus of $1000.

If we try to use `peter` to call the `calculatePerfBonus()` method, we'll get an error as the `BasicStaff` class does not have the `calculatePerfBonus()` method. Try adding the line

```
print('Peter\'s Performance Bonus = ',
peter.calculatePerfBonus())
```

to *inheritancedemo.py* and see what happens. You'll get an error message.

10.4 Python Special Methods

Now that we understand how inheritance and overriding works, let us move on to talk about special methods.

Previously, we mentioned in Chapter 9 that Python comes with a large number of special methods. These methods are *also known as* magic methods and are always surrounded by double underscores. Two of the magic methods that we have encountered so far are __init__ and __str__.

One of the magical properties of a special method is that you do not invoke it directly. For instance, when you wanted to print information about the instance officeStaff1 in Chapter 9, you do not write

```
print(officeStaff1.__str__())
```

Instead, you simply write

```
print(officeStaff1)
```

Python will invoke the necessary special method behind the scene.

Another property of special methods is that they can be overridden to suit our needs. The __str__ method is commonly overridden to provide a more human readable string representation of a class.

Other methods that are commonly overridden are the __add__, __sub__, __mul__ and __div__ methods. These methods allow us to modify standard operators such as the +, −, * and / signs so that they can do different things depending on what they are 'operating' on.

We have already encountered how the plus sign (+) can mean addition or concatenation. For instance, if we type

```
2+3
```

the + operator adds the two numbers to give us 5.

However, if we type

```
'Hello' + ' World'
```

the + operator concatenates the two strings to give us `'Hello World'`.

There is a special method for every operator sign. We can override the corresponding special method to provide even more meaning to them. This is known as overloading the operators. The special methods for +, −, *, / are __add__, __sub__, __mul__ and __div__ respectively.

Let's try to overload the + operator for our Staff class.

Add the following method to *classdemo.py*. We'll add this method to the Staff class so that both the child classes can use it.

```
def __add__(self, other):
    return self.pay + other.pay
```

This method overrides the __add__ method. It has two parameters self and other. self refers to one instance, `other` refers to another instance. It basically tells the compiler to add the `pay` variable of both instances and return the result.

To call the method, we use the + operator.

Add the following lines to *inheritancedemo.py*.

```
totalPay = john + peter
print('\nTotal Pay for Both Staff = ', totalPay)
```

Run the program and key in 120, 15, 150, 20 and A when prompted. You'll get the same output as the previous section, with one additional line shown below:

```
Total Pay for Both Staff =  5800
```

10.5 Python Built-in Functions for Objects

We've covered most of the topics in object-oriented programming. Before we end this chapter, let's look at some special built in functions that Python has for objects. To explore some of these functions, let's consider the two classes below. Create a new file in IDLE and name it *objectfunctions.py*. Copy the following code into the file:

```
class ParentClass:
    def __init__(self):
        self.a = 1
        print("Parent Class Object Created")
    def someMethod(self):
        print("Hello")

class ChildClass(ParentClass):
    def __init__(self):
        print("Child Class Object Created")

parent = ParentClass()
child = ChildClass()
```

Now, we are ready to test some of the built-in Python functions below. Run the file to try the following commands in Python Shell.

`isinstance()`

This function takes in two arguments. It checks if the first argument is an instance of the second argument (or an instance of a sub class of the second argument). The second argument can be a class or a built-in type in Python. It can also be a tuple consisting of more than one class or type.

If the second argument is not a valid class or type (or a tuple of classes or types), an exception is raised.

Try typing the following lines into Shell:

Example 1:

```
isinstance(parent, ParentClass)
```

Output:
You'll get `True` as `parent` is an instance of `ParentClass`

Example 2:

```
isinstance(5, int)
```

Output:
You'll get `True` as 5 is an instance of `int`. (`int` is a built-in type in Python for integers.)

Example 3:

```
isinstance(child, ParentClass)
```

Output:

You'll get `True` as `child` is an instance of `ChildClass`, which is a subclass of `ParentClass`.

Example 4:

```
isinstance(parent, (ParentClass, int))
```

Output:
You'll get `True` as `parent` is an instance of `ParentClass`, which is one of the types in the tuple `(ParentClass, int)`.

Example 5:

```
isinstance(parent, ChildClass)
```

Output:
You'll get `False` as an instance of the parent class is not considered an instance of the child class.

Example 6:

```
isinstance(parent, MyClass)
```

Output:
You'll get `NameError: name 'MyClass' is not defined` as `MyClass` is not a valid class. You can use the following code to manage such exceptions:

```
try:
    isinstance(parent, MyClass)
except NameError:
    print("No such class")
```

you'll get

```
No such class
```

as the output.

This function takes in two arguments – the name of two classes or types. It checks if the first argument is a subclass of the second argument. The second argument can be a tuple. The function returns `True` if the first argument is a subclass of any of the classes or types in the tuple. If the second argument is not a valid class or type, an exception is raised.

For instance, if you type

```
issubclass(ChildClass, ParentClass)
issubclass(ParentClass, ParentClass)
issubclass(ChildClass, int)
issubclass(ChildClass, (int, ParentClass))
```

you'll get

```
True
True
False
True
```

as the output. The second statement returns `True` as a class is considered a subclass of itself.

hasttr()

This function tests if an instance has a certain attribute. An attribute can refer to both data (variables) and methods. It takes in two arguments. The first is the name of the object and the second is the name of the attribute. The name of the attribute is in the form of a string and hence has to be enclosed with single quotes. For instance, if we add the following lines to Shell

```
hasattr(parent, 'a')
```

```
hasattr(parent, 'someMethod')
hasattr(parent, 'b')
```

we'll get

```
True
True
False
```

as the output. This is because `parent` has the attributes 'a' and `'someMethod'`, but does not have the attribute 'b'.

Project: Math and Binary

Congratulations! We've now covered enough fundamentals of Python (and programming in general) to start coding our first full program. In this chapter, we're going to code a simple console game that consists of two mini games – a Mathematics game and a Binary game.

At the start of the game, users can choose if they want to play the math or binary game. In addition, they'll also be prompted to enter the number of questions that they want for that round. They must choose to answer between 1 to 10 questions per round.

The math game tests our understanding of the BODMAS rule of arithmetic calculation. If you are unsure what BODMAS is, you can check out this site http://www.mathsisfun.com/operation-order-bodmas.html.

The binary game, on the other hand, requires players to convert a base 10 number to a binary (base 2) number. If you are new to binary numbers, check out this article http://www.mathsisfun.com/binary-number-system.html

In both cases, the game randomly sets a question for players to answer. If they get the answer wrong, the program will display the correct answer and proceed to the next question. If they get it correct, the program will update their scores and proceed to the next question.

The program keeps track of the players' scores and saves those scores in an external text file. After each round, players can key "-1" to terminate the program or press Enter to start a new round.

I've broken down the program into small exercises so that you can try coding the program yourself. Try the exercises before referring to the answers. Answers are provided in Appendix E or you can go to http://www.learncodingfast.com/python to download the Python files. I would strongly encourage you to download the source code as the formatting in Appendix E may result in the distortion of some indentation which makes the code difficult to read.

Remember, learning the Python syntax is easy but boring. Problem solving is where the fun lies. If you encounter difficulties when doing these exercises, try harder. This is where the reward is the greatest.

Ready? Let's go!

Part 1: gametasks.py

We will be writing three files for our programs: *gametasks.py*, *gameclasses.py* and *project.py*. Part 1 will focus on writing the code for *gametasks.py*.

To start, let's first create a new file in IDLE and name it *gametasks.py*.

gametasks.py is a module that contains three functions that perform certain tasks in our project. These functions do not require any information about an instance or a class and are thus not written as part of a class.

Exercise 1.1: Print Game Instructions

The first function is called `printInstructions()`. It has one parameter called `instruction` and simply uses the built-in `print()` function to print the value of `instruction` onto the display. Try coding this function yourself.

Exercise 1.2: Getting the User's Score

The second function is called `getUserScore()`. This function accepts one parameter, `userName`.

The function first opens a file called *userScores.txt* in `'r'` mode.

userScores.txt looks something like this:

Ann, 100
Benny, 102
Carol, 214
Darren, 129

Each line records the information of one user. The first value is the user's username and the second is the user's score.

Next, the function reads the file line by line using a `for` loop.

Within the `for` loop, each line is split using the `split()` function (refer to Appendix A for an example on using the `split()` function) and the results of the `split()` function is stored in a list called `content`. Try coding this first.

Next, still within the `for` loop, the function checks if any of the lines has the same username as the value that is passed in as the parameter. If there is, the function closes the file and returns the score beside that username.

After looping through the file, if the function does not find a match for the username, it exits the `for` loop, closes the file and returns the string "-1".

Clear so far? Try coding this function.

Done?

Now we need to make some modifications to our code. When opening our file previously, we used the `'r'` mode. This helps to prevent any accidental changes to the file. However, when opening a file in `'r'` mode, an `IOError` occurs if the file does not already exist. Hence when we run the program for the first time, we'll end up with an error since the file *userScores.txt* does not exist previously. To prevent this error, we can do either of the following:

Instead of opening the file in `'r'` mode, we can open it in `'w'` mode. When opening in `'w'` mode, a new file will be created if the file does not exist previously. The risk with this method is we may accidentally write to the file, which results in all previous content being erased. However, since our program is a small program, we can check through our code carefully to prevent any accidental writing.

The second method is to use a `try, except` statement to handle the `IOError`. To do that, we need to put all our previous codes in the `try` block, then use `except IOError:` to handle the 'File not found' error. In the `except` block, we'll inform users that the file is not found and then proceed to create the file. We'll use the `open()` function with `'w'` mode to create it. The difference here is we use the `'w'` mode only when the file is not found. Since the file does not exist initially, there is no risk of erasing any previous content. After creating the file, we close the file and return the string "-1".

Try doing this yourself. You can choose either of the above methods to complete this exercise. The answer provided uses the second method. Once you are done, we can move on to Exercise 1.3.

Exercise 1.3: Updating the User's Score

In this exercise, we'll define another function called `updateUserScore()`.

This function requires us to use two built-in functions from the `os` module: the `remove()` and `rename()` functions.

Try importing these two functions yourself.

Done? Let's move on.

The `updateUserScore()` function has three parameters: `newUser`, `userName` and `score`. Let's add these parameters to the function definition.

`newUser` can either be `True` or `False`.

If `newUser` is `True`, the function will open the file `userScores.txt` in <u>append</u> mode and add the user's `userName` and `score` to the file using the `write()` function. After that, it'll close the file. Try coding this `if` block yourself.

Else, if `newUser` is `False`, the function will <u>update</u> the user's score in the file. However, there is no function in Python (or most programming languages for that matter) that allows us to update a text file. We can only write or append to it, but we cannot update it.

Hence, we need to create a temporary file. This is a fairly common practice in programming. Let's call this file *userScores.tmp*. Recall that we can create a new file by opening it in `'w'` mode. Let's create the file now. We need to create it inside the `else` block.

Done?

Now, still within the `else` block, let's open the *userScores.txt* file in `'r'` mode as we will only be reading from it. Next, we need to loop through *userScores.txt* line by line using a `for` loop and split the line using the `split()` function. We assign the result of the `split()` function to a list called `content`.

For each line, we check if the username on that line is the same as the one provided by the parameter `userName`. If it is, we'll change the score to the new score provided by the parameter `score` and write this updated line to the *userScores.tmp* file.

If it is not the same, we'll simply write the original line to the temporary file *userScores.tmp*.

For instance, if the arguments provided to the function are `False`, `'Benny'` and `'158'` (i.e. `updateUserScore(False, 'Benny', '158')`), the table below shows the difference between the original *userScores.txt* and the new *userScores.tmp* file.

userScores.txt

Ann, 100
Benny, 102
Carol, 214
Darren, 129

userScores.tmp

Ann, 100
Benny, 158
Carol, 214
Darren, 129

Try doing this step yourself.

Once we are done with that, we exit the `for` loop and close both files. We then delete *userScores.txt*. Finally, we rename *userScores.tmp* to *userScores.txt*.

Clear? Try coding the `else` block yourself.

Once you are done, the `updateUserScore()` function is complete. This also marks the end of the *gametasks.py* file.

Part 2: gameclasses.py

Exercise 2.1: The Game class

We've now come to the second part of the project. In this section, we'll code a new file that contains three classes: `Game`, `MathGame` and `BinaryGame`.

Create a new file in IDLE and name it *gameclasses.py*.

We'll start with the `Game` class. This class is a very simple class from which two other classes will be derived.

The class has one initializer with two parameters: `self` and `noOfQuestions`. `noOfQuestions` has a default value of zero.

Within the initializer, we assign `noOfQuestions` to an <u>instance variable</u> called `_noOfQuestions`. Try defining the initializer and adding this assignment statement yourself.

Done?

Besides the initializer, the `Game` class also has a property for getting and setting the value of `_noOfQuestion`. The code for the getter method is shown below:

```
@property
def noOfQuestions(self):
    return self._noOfQuestions
```

As you can see, the getter method simply returns the value of `_noOfQuestions`.

The setter method, on the other hand, is more complex. It has two parameters – `self` and `value`.

If `value` is less than one, the setter method sets `_noOfQuestions` to 1 and prints the messages "`Minimum Number of Questions = 1`" and "`Hence, number of questions will be set to 1`".

If `value` is more than ten, the setter method sets `_noOfQuestions` to 10 and prints the messages "`Maximum Number of Questions = 10`" and "`Hence, number of questions will be set to 10`".

If neither of the above applies, the setter method sets `_noOfQuestions` to `value`. Try coding the setter method yourself.

Once you are done, the `Game` class is complete.

Exercise 2.2: The BinaryGame class

Next, let's move on to the `BinaryGame` class. This class derives from the `Game` class. Try defining the `BinaryGame` class yourself.

The `BinaryGame` class only has one method called `generateQuestions()`. This is an <u>instance method</u> and is responsible for generating binary questions. Specifically, the method presents the player with a base-10 number and requires the player to convert the number to a base-2 number. For instance, the method may give the player the number 12. The player is then required to convert the number to 1100, which is the base-2 equivalent of the number 12.

The structure of the `generateQuestions()` method is as follows:

```
def generateQuestions(self):

    #import randint
```

```
#declare local variable called score
#use for loop to generate questions and
evaluate answers
#return the value of score
```

(a) Importing the `randint()` function

As shown in the structure above, to generate the questions, we need to first import the `randint()` function from the `random` module. The `randint()` function generates a random integer within the range provided by us. We'll use that to generate numbers for our questions later. Try importing the function yourself.

(b) Declaring variables

Next, we need to declare a local variable called `score`. This variable is used to store the score of the player during the game. Try declaring this variable and initializing it to zero.

(c) Generating questions

After this, we are ready to generate the questions. The number of questions generated by the function depends on the instance variable `_noOfQuestions` that `BinaryGame` inherited from `Game`. We'll use the getter method to get this variable. To control the number of questions generated, we'll use a `for` loop. Here's how the `for` loop looks like:

```
for i in range(self.noOfQuestions):
```

Within the `for` loop, we use the `randint()` function to generate a random number. The `randint()` function has two parameters, `start` and `end`, and returns a random integer N such that $start <= N <= end$.

For instance, if `randint(1, 9)` is called, it'll randomly return an integer from the numbers 1, 2, 3, 4, 5, 6, 7, 8, 9.

For our function, we'll use `randint()` to generate a number from 1 to 100 and assign the result to a local variable called `base10`.

Next, we need to use the `input()` function to prompt the user to convert the number to binary. We'll then assign the user's answer to a local variable called `userResult`.

Try doing these steps yourself.

Next, still within the `for` loop, we need to compare the user's input with the correct answer. We'll do that using a `while True` loop. A `while True` loop is basically a loop that runs indefinitely. This is because writing `while True` is equivalent to writing something like `while 1==1`. Since 1 is always equals to 1 (hence always `True`), the `while` condition will never evaluate to `False`. Hence, the loop will run indefinitely. In order to exit the loop, we need to use a `break` statement.

Here's a suggestion on how you can use a `while True` loop for this exercise.

```
while True:
    try:
        #cast user's answer to an integer and
evaluate the answer
        #update user score based on the answer
        #break out from the while True loop
using the break statement
    except:
        #print error message if casting fails
        #prompt user to key in the answer again
```

Recall that the `input()` function returns user input as a string? Within the `while True` loop, we use a `try, except` statement to try casting the input into a number. If the cast fails, the program should inform the user of the error and prompt the user to type in a valid input.

The `while True` loop will keep looping until the `try` block executes correctly and reaches the `break` statement.

Let's work on the `try` block.

We'll be using the built-in `int()` function to try casting the user's input into an integer. However, we need to inform Python that the number that we are trying to cast is a base-2 number. This can be achieved with the code below:

```
answer = int(userResult, base = 2)
```

When we write `base = 2` within the parentheses for the `int()` function, Python knows that `userResult` is meant to be interpreted as a base-2 number.

`int()` then converts the string into a base-10 integer and returns the value. We can then assign it to a local variable called `answer`.

Next, we use an `if` statement to compare `answer` with the original base-10 number (which is stored in the variable `base10`).

If the two values are the same, we inform the user that the answer is correct and add 1 to the value of `score`. We then use the `break` keyword to exit the `while True` loop.

If the user gets it wrong, we'll inform the user and display the correct answer. To do that, we can use the `format()` method covered in Chapter 4.3. To display a number in binary form, we need to use the `b` formatter as shown below:

```
print("Wrong answer. The correct answer is
{:b}.".format(base10))
```

After displaying the answer, we'll use the `break` keyword to exit the `while True` loop too. With that, the `try` block is complete. Try coding the `try` block yourself.

Next, let us move on to the `except` block. This block is executed if the `int()` function fails to convert the user's input into a number. Inside the `except` block, we inform the user that he/she did not enter a binary number and use the `input()` function to prompt the user to enter a new number. We then use this new input to update the variable `userResult`. With that, the `except` block is complete.

(d) Returning value of `score`

After we exit the `except` block, we exit the `while True` loop and `for` loop as well. At this stage, the function has finished generating all the necessary questions. Now we simply return the value of `score`.

Try coding this function yourself. Once you finish coding the `generateQuestions()` function, the `BinaryGame` class is done and we are ready to move on to the `MathGame` class.

Exercise 2.3: The MathGame class

The `MathGame` class is very similar to the `BinaryGame` class. It also derives from the `Game` class. Try defining the class yourself.

Within the `MathGame` class, we only have one method called `generateQuestions()`. The basic structure of the `generateQuestions()` method is similar to that in the `BinaryGame` class:

```
def generateQuestions(self):

    #import randint
    #declare four local variables called score,
numberList, symbolList and operatorDict
    #use for loop to generate questions and
evaluate answers
    #return the value of score
```

(a) Importing the `randint()` function

As before, to generate the questions, we need to first import the `randint()` function from the `random` module. Try importing this function yourself.

(b) Declaring variables

Next, we need to declare four local variables. The first variable is called `score`. This is used to store the score of the player. We initialize it to zero.

After this, we need two lists. We shall name the two lists `numberList` and `symbolList`.

`numberList` should store five numbers, with 0 as their initial values. `symbolList` should store four strings, with ' ' as their initial values.

Finally, we need a dictionary. The dictionary consists of 4 pairs, with integers 1 to 4 as the dictionary keys, and "+", "-", "*", "**" as the data. Let's call this `operatorDict`.

Try declaring and initializing the variables yourself.

(c) Generating questions

Done? Now we are ready to generate the questions. The number of questions generated by the function depends on the instance variable _noOfQuestions that MathGame inherited from Game. Try defining a for loop to achieve this. You can refer to the generateQuestions() function in BinaryGame for reference.

Done? Now, let us work on the for loop.

Within the for loop, we need to update numberList with random numbers. To do that, we use the randint() function to generate a random number from 1 to 9. We can do this one by one since numberList only has five members. We can write

```
numberList[0] = randint(1, 9)
numberList[1] = randint(1, 9)
numberList[2] = randint(1, 9)
numberList[3] = randint(1, 9)
numberList[4] = randint(1, 9)
```

Each time randint(1, 9) is called, it'll randomly return an integer from the numbers 1, 2, 3, 4, 5, 6, 7, 8, 9.

However, this is not the most elegant way of updating our numberList. Imagine how cumbersome it'll be if numberList has 1000 members. The better alternative is to use a for loop.

Try using a for loop to accomplish the task. (Note: Here we are using a for loop inside another for loop)

Done? Great!

Now that we have the numbers to operate on, we need to randomly generate the mathematical symbols (+, -, *, **) for our questions. To do that, we'll use the randint() function and the operatorDict dictionary.

`randint()` will generate the dictionary key, which will then be mapped to the correct operator using the `operatorDict` dictionary. For instance, to assign a symbol to `symbolList[0]`, we write

```
symbolList[0] = operatorDict[randint(1, 4)]
```

Similar to `numberList`, you should use a `for` loop to complete this task. However, there is one problem that makes this `for` loop harder than the previous one.

Recall that in Python, ** stands for exponent (i.e. 2**3 = 2^3)?

The problem is, when we have two consecutive exponent operators in Python, such as 2**3**2, Python interprets it as 2**(3**2) instead of (2**3)**2. In the first case, the answer is 2 to the power of 9 (i.e. 2^9) which is 512. In the second case, the answer is 8 to the power of 2 (i.e. 8^2) which is 64. Hence when we present a question like 2**3**2, the user will get the answer wrong if he interprets it as (2**3)**2.

To prevent this problem, we're going to modify our code so that we do not get two consecutive ** signs. In other words, `symbolList = ['+', '+', '-', '**']` is fine but `symbolList = ['+', '-', '**', '**']` is not.

This exercise is the hardest among all the exercises. Try coming up with a solution to prevent two consecutive ** signs. Once you are done, we can proceed on to the next step.

Hint: If you are stuck, you can consider using an `if` statement within the `for` loop.

Now that we have our symbols and numbers, we are going to try to generate the mathematical expression as a string. This expression uses the five numbers from `numberList` and the four mathematical symbols from `symbolList` to form a question.

We have to declare another variable called `questionString` and assign the mathematical expression to `questionString`. Examples of `questionString` include

$6 - 2*3 - 2**1$
$4 + 5 - 2*6 + 1$
$8 - 0*2 + 5 - 8$

Try to generate this expression yourself.

Hint: You can first assign the first item in `numberList` to `questionString` and then use a `for` loop to concatenate the remaining items from `numberList` and `symbolList` to get the mathematical expression. Note that you need to cast items in `numberList` into a string first (using the built-in `str()` function) before concatenating them with other strings.

Try doing this yourself.

Done? Good! We should now have a mathematical expression as a string, assigned to the variable `questionString`. To evaluate the result of this expression, we're going to use a brilliant built-in function that comes with Python, `eval()`.

`eval()` interprets a string as a code and executes the code. For instance, if we write `eval("1+2+4")`, we'll get the number 7.

Hence to evaluate the result of our mathematical expression, we pass in `questionString` to the `eval()` function and assign the result to a new variable named `result`.

Try doing this yourself.

Now, we need to display the question to the user. As mentioned earlier, in Python, the ** symbol stands for exponent. That is, 2**3 = 8. However, to most users, ** has no meaning. Hence if we display a question as 2**3 + 8 - 5, the user will likely be confused. To prevent that, we'll replace any ** symbol in `questionString` with the ^ symbol.

To do that, we'll use the built-in function `replace()`. Using it is pretty straightforward, just write `questionString = questionString.replace("**", "^")`.

After replacing the original question string to a more reader-friendly string, we use the `input()` function to prompt the user to evaluate the question and assign the result to a local variable called `userResult`.

Now, we are ready to evaluate the answer and update the user's score. Similar to what we did for the `BinaryGame` class, we'll use a `while True` loop to repeatedly prompt the user for an answer if he/she fails to enter a value that can be converted to an integer using the `int()` function.

On the other hand, if the user enters a valid value, we'll compare it with the correct answer (which is stored in `result`). If the two values are the same, we inform the user that the answer is correct and add 1 to the value of `score`. We then use the `break` keyword to exit the `while True` loop.

If the user gets it wrong, we'll inform the user and display the correct answer. After that, we'll use the `break` keyword to exit the `while True` loop.

Try coding this `while True` loop yourself. It is almost identical to the `while True` loop in the `BinaryGame` class. You can refer to that if you are stuck.

(d) Returning value of `score`

Done? Once you are done with the `while True` loop, you can exit both the `while True` loop and `for` loop and return the local variable `score`. This marks the end of the `generateQuestions()` method and also the end of the `MathGame` class.

With that, the *gameclasses.py* file is complete.

Part 3: project.py

Congratulations for completing Part 1 and 2.

Part 3 is going to be relatively easy as we'll mainly be calling the functions and methods that we defined earlier. Let's start now by creating a new file called *project.py*.

Exercise 3.1: Importing classes and functions

First, we need to import the classes and functions that we coded in the previous two files. Try doing this yourself.

Next, we are ready to start coding the main program. We'll enclose our main program in a `try, except` statement. We want to handle any unforeseen errors when running the main program. The structure for the `try, except` statement is as follows:

```
try:
    #declare variables
    #use a while loop to run the program until
the user chooses to exit
    #update the user's score after he/she exits
the program
except Exception as e:
```

```
#inform users that an error has occurred and
the program will exit
```

Exercise 3.2: Writing the try block

We'll start with the code for the `try` block.

(a) Declaring variables

Let's declare two local variables called `mathInstructions`
and `binaryInstructions`. As the names suggest, these are
variables that store instructions for the two games. The
instructions for the math game is as follows:

```
In this game, you will be given a simple
arithmetic question.
Each correct answer gives you one mark.
No mark is deducted for wrong answers.
```

The instructions for the binary game is as follows:

```
In this game, you will be given a number in base
10.
Your task is to convert this number to base 2.
Each correct answer gives you one mark.
No mark is deducted for wrong answers.
```

Try declaring the two variables yourself and assigning the two
strings to the correct variable.

Next, we shall instantiate two objects called `bg` and `mg`, which
are instances of the `BinaryGame` and `MathGame` classes
respectively.

After that, we need to prompt the user for his/her username and
assign the value to the variable `userName`. Once we are done,
we pass this variable to the function `getUserScore()`.

`getUserScore()` will either return the score of the user or return '-1' (if the user is not found). Let's cast this result into an integer and assign it to a variable called `score`.

Next, we need to set the value of another variable called `newUser`. If `score` is -1, we set `newUser` to `True` and change the value of `score` from -1 to 0. Else, we set `newUser` to `False`.

Try coding this yourself.

Once you are done with it, we'll print a message on the screen to welcome the user and display his score.

(b) Using a `while` loop to run the program

The next part of our program involves a `while` loop. Specifically, our program will prompt for input from our user to determine if it should terminate the program or do something else.

You need to declare another variable `userChoice` and give it an initial value of 0.

Next, using a `while` loop, we compare `userChoice` with a string of your choice, say "-1". If `userChoice` is not the same as "-1", the game keeps running until `userChoice` becomes "-1".

The structure of the while loop is as follows:

```
userChoice = 0

while userChoice != '-1'
    #prompt user to select Math game or Binary
game
    #prompt user for number of questions per
game
```

```
    #display relevant questions based on user's
selection and update user's score
    #display updated score to user
    #prompt user to enter a choice again and use
it to update userChoice
```

Within the `while` loop, we do a few things.

First, we prompt the user to choose between a Math game or a Binary game using the following prompt message:

```
Math Game (1) or Binary Game (2)?
```

Next, we assign the user's input to a local variable called `game` and use a `while` loop to keep prompting the user for a valid choice if the user did not enter '1' or '2'. Here, we are using a `while` loop inside another `while` loop. The inner `while` loop is controlled by the variable `game` while the outer `while` loop is controlled by the variable `userChoice`.

Try coding this inner `while` loop yourself. Remember to update the variable `game` inside the inner `while` loop so that you do not get an infinite loop.

Once you are done with that, we go on to prompt the user to enter the number of questions that he/she wants for that game and assign the user's input to `numPrompt`. We'll use the prompt below:

```
How many questions do you want per game (1 to
10)?
```

Next, we need to try casting `numPrompt` into an integer. To do that, we use a `while True` loop similar to what we used in Exercise 2.2 and 2.3 for the `generateQuestions()` method. The structure of the `while True` loop is as follows:

```
while True:
    try:
        #cast numPrompt into an integer and
assign it to a local variable called num.
        #break
    except:
        #notify user that they did not enter a
valid number
        #prompt user to enter the number of
questions again and assign the result to
numPrompt.
```

Try coding this `while True` loop yourself.

Once you are done with that, we are ready to display the relevant questions based on the user's choice.

We'll use an `if` statement for this.

If user chose to play a Math game (i.e. `game == '1'`), we do three things:

First, we use the statement below to set the value of the instance variable `_noOfQuestions` in the `MathGame` class.

```
mg.noOfQuestions = num
```

Here, we are using the setter method inside the `MathGame` class to set the value of `_noOfQuestions`. This prevents the user from setting a value that is greater than 10 or smaller than 1.

Next, we use the `printInstructions()` function to print the instructions for the Math game.

Finally, we use `mg` to call the `generateQuestions()` method in the `MathGame` class. This method generates the relevant questions and returns the score that the user got for that round. We add this value to the existing value of `score` to update it.

Try coding the above three steps yourself.

Once you are done, you can move on to the `else` block.

This block is very similar to the `if` block except that we use `bg` instead of `mg` to call the methods in the `BinaryGame` class. Try coding the `else` block yourself.

After all the questions are displayed, we display the current score to the user.

Next, we prompt the user to press Enter to continue or "-1" to exit and use the result to update `userChoice`.

With that, we can exit the `while` loop.

(c) Updating *userScores.txt*

Once we are outside the `while` loop, we need to update the *userScores.txt* file. To do that, we simply call the `updateUserScore()` function by passing in the variables `newUser`, `userName` and `score`. We need to cast `score` into a string (using the `str()` function) as the `updateUserScore()` function requires `score` to be a string so that it can be concatenated with other strings inside the function.

That's all for the `try` block.

Exercise 3.3: Writing the except block

Now, let's move on to the `except` block. For the `except` block, we inform the user that an unknown error has occurred and the program will exit. In addition, we also print out the system generated error message to get a brief description of what the error is.

With that, the program is complete!!! That's it, you have just finished coding your first program in Python. Excited? I sure hope you are as excited about it as I am. :)

Now try running the program `project.py`. Does it work as expected?

If your code does not work, compare it with the sample answer and try to figure out what went wrong. You'll learn a lot by analyzing your mistakes. Problem solving is where the fun lies and where the reward is the greatest. Have fun and never give up! The sample answer can be found in Appendix E.

Thank You

We've come to the end of the book. Thank you for reading this book and I hope you have enjoyed the book. More importantly, I sincerely hope the book has helped you master the fundamentals of Python programming.

I know you could have picked from a dozen of books on Python Programming, but you took a chance with this book. Thank you once again for downloading this book and reading all the way to the end. Please do try the exercises and challenges. You'll learn a lot by doing.

Now I'd like to ask for a "small" favor. Could you please take a few minutes or two to leave a review for this book on Amazon?

This feedback will help me tremendously and will help me continue to write more guides on programming. If you like the book or have any suggestions for improvement, please let me know. I will be deeply grateful. :)

Last but not least, remember you can download the source code for the project and the appendices at http://www.learncodingfast.com/python.

You can also contact me at jamie@learncodingfast.com.

Appendix A: Working With Strings

Note: The notation [start, [end]] means *start* and *end* are optional. If only one number is provided, it is taken to be *start*.

\# marks the start of a comment
''' marks the start and end of a multiline comment
The actual code is in monotype font.
=> marks the start of the output

count (sub, [start, [end]])

Returns the number of times the substring *sub* appears in the string.
This function is case-sensitive.

[Example]

```
# In the examples below, 's' occurs at index 3, 6
and 10

# count the entire string
'This is a string'.count('s')
=> 3

# count from index 4 to end of string
'This is a string'.count('s', 4)
=> 2

# count from index 4 to 10-1
'This is a string'.count('s', 4, 10 )
=> 1

# count 'T'. There's only 1 'T' as the function is
case sensitive.
'This is a string'.count('T')
=> 1
```

endswith (suffix, [start, [end]])

Returns True if the string ends with the specified *suffix*,
otherwise returns False.
suffix can also be a tuple of suffixes to look for.
This function is case-sensitive.

[Example]

```
# 'man' occurs at index 4 to 6

# check the entire string
'Postman'.endswith('man')
=> True

# check from index 3 to end of string
'Postman'.endswith('man', 3)
=> True

# check from index 2 to 6-1
'Postman'.endswith('man', 2, 6)
=> False

# check from index 2 to 7-1
'Postman'.endswith('man', 2, 7)
=> True

# Using a tuple of suffixes (check from index 2
to 6-1)
'Postman'.endswith(('man', 'ma'), 2, 6)
=> True
```

find/index (sub, [start, [end]])

Returns the index in the string where the first occurrence of the
substring *sub* is found.
find() returns -1 if *sub* is not found.

index() returns ValueError if *sub* is not found.
This function is case-sensitive.

[Example]

```
# check the entire string
'This is a string'.find('s')
=> 3

# check from index 4 to end of string
'This is a string'.find('s', 4)
=> 6

# check from index 7 to 11-1
'This is a string'.find('s', 7,11 )
=> 10

# sub is not found
'This is a string'.find('p')
=> -1

'This is a string'.index('p')
=> ValueError
```

isalnum()

Returns True if all characters in the string are alphanumeric and there is at least one character, False otherwise.
Alphanumeric does not include whitespaces.

[Example]

```
'abcd1234'.isalnum()
=> True

'a b c d 1 2 3 4'.isalnum()
=> False
```

```
'abcd'.isalnum()
=> True

'1234'.isalnum()
=> True
```

isalpha()

Returns True if all characters in the string are alphabetic and there is at least one character, False otherwise.

[Example]

```
'abcd'.isalpha()
=> True

'abcd1234'.isalpha()
=> False

'1234'.isalpha()
=> False

'a b c'.isalpha()
=> False
```

isdigit()

Returns True if all characters in the string are digits and there is at least one character, False otherwise.

[Example]

```
'1234'.isdigit()
=> True

'abcd1234'.isdigit()
=> False
```

```
'abcd'.isdigit()
=> False

'1 2 3 4'.isdigit()
=> False
```

islower()

Returns `True` if all cased characters in the string are lowercase and there is at least one cased character, `False` otherwise.

[Example]

```
'abcd'.islower()
=> True

'Abcd'.islower()
=> False

'ABCD'.islower()
=> False
```

isspace()

Returns `True` if there are only whitespace characters in the string and there is at least one character, `False` otherwise.

[Example]

```
' '.isspace()
=> True

'a b'.isspace()
=> False
```

istitle()

Returns `True` if the string is a titlecased string and there is at least one character

[Example]

```
'This Is A String'.istitle()
=> True

'This is a string'.istitle()
=> False
```

isupper()

Returns `True` if all cased characters in the string are uppercase and there is at least one cased character, `False` otherwise.

[Example]

```
'ABCD'.isupper()
=> True

'Abcd'.isupper()
=> False

'abcd'.isupper()
=> False
```

join()

Returns a string in which the argument provided is joined by a separator.

[Example]

```
sep = '-'
myTuple = ('a', 'b', 'c')
```

```
myList = ['d', 'e', 'f']
myString = "Hello World"

sep.join(myTuple)
=> 'a-b-c'

sep.join(myList)
=> 'd-e-f'

sep.join(myString)
=> 'H-e-l-l-o- -W-o-r-l-d''
```

lower()

Returns a copy of the string converted to lowercase.

[Example]

```
'Hello Python'.lower()
=> 'hello python'
```

replace(old, new[, count])

Returns a copy of the string with all occurrences of substring old replaced by new.
count is optional. If given, only the first count occurrences are replaced.
This function is case-sensitive.

[Example]

```
# Replace all occurences
'This is a string'.replace('s', 'p')
=> 'Thip ip a ptring'

# Replace first 2 occurences
'This is a string'.replace('s', 'p', 2)
=> 'Thip ip a string'
```

split([sep [,maxsplit]])

Returns a list of the words in the string, using *sep* as the delimiter string.
sep and *maxsplit* are optional.
If *sep* is not given, whitespace is used as the delimiter.
If *maxsplit* is given, at most *maxsplit* splits are done.
This function is case-sensitive.

[Example]

```
# Split using whitespace as delimiter
'This is a string'.split()
=> ['This', 'is', 'a', 'string']

# Split using comma followed by a whitespace as
the delimiter
'This, is, a, string'.split(', ')
=> ['This', 'is', 'a', 'string']

# Split using comma followed by a whitespace as
the delimiter
# Only do 2 splits
'This, is, a, string'.split(', ', 2)
=> ['This', 'is', 'a, string']
```

splitlines ([keepends])

Returns a list of the lines in the string, breaking at line boundaries.
Line breaks are not included in the resulting list unless *keepends* is given and `True`.

[Example]

```
# Split lines separated by \n
'This is the first line.\nThis is the second
line'.splitlines()
```

```
=> ['This is the first line.', 'This is the
second line.']

# Split multi line string (e.g. string that uses
the ''' mark)
'''This is the first line.
This is the second line.'''.splitlines()
=> ['This is the first line.', 'This is the
second line.']

# Split and keep line breaks
'This is the first line.\nThis is the second
line.'.splitlines(True)
=> ['This is the first line.\n', 'This is the
second line.']

'''This is the first line.
This is the second line.'''.splitlines(True)
=> ['This is the first line.\n', 'This is the
second line.']
```

startswith (prefix[, start[, end]])

Returns `True` if string starts with the prefix, otherwise returns `False`.
prefix can also be a tuple of prefixes to look for.
This function is case-sensitive.

[Example]

```
# 'Post' occurs at index 0 to 3

# check the entire string
'Postman'.startswith('Post')
=> True
```

```
# check from index 3 to end of string
'Postman'.startswith('Post', 3)
=> False

# check from index 2 to 6-1
'Postman'.startswith('Post', 2, 6)
=> False

# check from index 2 to 6-1
'Postman'.startswith('stm', 2, 6)
=> True

# Using a tuple of prefixes (check from index 3
to end of string)
'Postman'.startswith(('Post', 'tma'), 3)
=> True
```

strip ([chars])

Returns a copy of the string with the leading and trailing characters *char* removed.
If *char* is not provided, whitespaces will be removed.
This function is case-sensitive.

[Example]

```
# Strip whitespaces
'   This is a string   '.strip()
=> 'This is a string'

# Strip 's'. Nothing is removed since 's' is not
at the start or end of the string
'This is a string'.strip('s')
=> 'This is a string'

# Strip 'g'.
'This is a string'.strip('g')
=> 'This is a strin'
```

upper()

Returns a copy of the string converted to uppercase.

[Example]

```
'Hello Python'.upper()
=> 'HELLO PYTHON'
```

Appendix B: Working With Lists

=> marks the start of the output

append( )

Add item to the end of a list

[Example]

```
myList = ['a', 'b', 'c', 'd']
myList.append('e')
print (myList)
=> ['a', 'b', 'c', 'd', 'e']
```

del

Remove items from a list

[Example]

```
myList = ['a', 'b', 'c', 'd', 'e', 'f', 'g',
'h', 'i', 'j', 'k', 'l']

#delete the third item (index = 2)
del myList[2]
print (myList)
=> ['a', 'b', 'd', 'e', 'f', 'g', 'h', 'i', 'j',
'k', 'l']

#delete items from index 1 to 5-1
del myList[1:5]
print (myList)
=> ['a', 'g', 'h', 'i', 'j', 'k', 'l']

#delete items from index 0 to 3-1
del myList [ :3]
```

```
print (myList)
=> ['i', 'j', 'k', 'l']

#delete items from index 2 to end
del myList [2:]
print (myList)
=> ['i', 'j']
```

extend( )

Combine two lists

[Example]

```
myList = ['a', 'b', 'c', 'd', 'e']
myList2 = [1, 2, 3, 4]
myList.extend(myList2)
print (myList)
=> ['a', 'b', 'c', 'd', 'e', 1, 2, 3, 4]
```

in

Check if an item is in a list

[Example]

```
myList = ['a', 'b', 'c', 'd']
'c' in myList
=> True

'e' in myList
=> False
```

insert( )

Add item to a list at a particular position

[Example]

```
myList = ['a', 'b', 'c', 'd', 'e']
myList.insert(1, 'Hi')
print (myList)
=> ['a', 'Hi', 'b', 'c', 'd', 'e']
```

len( )

Find the number of items in a list

[Example]

```
myList = ['a', 'b', 'c', 'd']
print (len(myList))
=> 4
```

pop( )

Get the value of an item and remove it from the list
Requires index of item as the argument

[Example]

```
myList = ['a', 'b', 'c', 'd', 'e']

#remove the third item
member = myList.pop(2)
print (member)
=> c

print (myList)
=> ['a', 'b', 'd', 'e']

#remove the last item
member = myList.pop( )
print (member)
=> e
```

```
print (myList)
=> ['a', 'b', 'd']
```

remove( )

Remove an item from a list. Requires the value of the item as the argument.

[Example]

```
myList = ['a', 'b', 'c', 'd', 'e']

#remove the item 'c'
myList.remove('c')
print (myList)
=> ['a', 'b', 'd', 'e']
```

reverse()

Reverse the items in a list

[Example]

```
myList = [1, 2, 3, 4]
myList.reverse()
print (myList)
=> [4, 3, 2, 1]
```

sort()

Sort a list alphabetically or numerically

[Example]

```
myList = [3, 0, -1, 4, 6]
myList.sort()
print(myList)
=> [-1, 0, 3, 4, 6]
```

sorted()

Returns a new sorted list without sorting the original list.
Requires a list as the argument

[Example]

```
myList = [3, 0, -1, 4, 6]
myList2 = sorted(myList)

#Original list is not sorted
print (myList)
=> [3, 0, -1, 4, 6]

#New list is sorted
print (myList2)
=> [-1, 0, 3, 4, 6]
```

Addition Operator: +

Concatenate List

[Example]

```
myList = ['a', 'b', 'c', 'd']
print (myList + ['e', 'f'])
=> ['a', 'b', 'c', 'd', 'e', 'f']

print (myList)
=> ['a', 'b', 'c', 'd']
```

Multiplication Operator: *

Duplicate a list and concatenate it to the end of the list

[Example]

```
myList = ['a', 'b', 'c', 'd']
```

```
print (myList*3)
=> ['a', 'b', 'c', 'd', 'a', 'b', 'c', 'd', 'a',
'b', 'c', 'd']

print (myList)
=> ['a', 'b', 'c', 'd']
```

Note:
The + and * symbols do not modify the list. The list stays as ['a', 'b', 'c', 'd'] in both cases.

Appendix C: Working With Tuples

=> marks the start of the output

del

Delete the entire tuple

[Example]

```
myTuple = ('a', 'b', 'c', 'd')
del myTuple
print (myTuple)
=> NameError: name 'myTuple' is not defined
```

in

Check if an item is in a tuple

[Example]

```
myTuple = ('a', 'b', 'c', 'd')
'c' in myTuple
=> True

'e' in myTuple
=> False
```

len( )

Find the number of items in a tuple

[Example]

```
myTuple = ('a', 'b', 'c', 'd')
print (len(myTuple))
=> 4
```

Addition Operator: +

Concatenate Tuples

[Example]

```
myTuple = ('a', 'b', 'c', 'd')
print (myTuple + ('e', 'f'))
=> ('a', 'b', 'c', 'd', 'e', 'f')

print (myTuple)
=> ('a', 'b', 'c', 'd')
```

Multiplication Operator: *

Duplicate a tuple and concatenate it to the end of the tuple

[Example]

```
myTuple = ('a', 'b', 'c', 'd')
print(myTuple*3)
=> ('a', 'b', 'c', 'd', 'a', 'b', 'c', 'd', 'a',
'b', 'c', 'd')

print (myTuple)
=> ('a', 'b', 'c', 'd')
```

Note: The + and * symbols do not modify the tuple. The tuple stays as ['a', 'b', 'c', 'd'] in both cases.

Appendix D: Working With Dictionaries

=> marks the start of the output

clear( )

Removes all elements of the dictionary, returning an empty dictionary

[Example]

```
dic1 = {1: 'one', 2: 'two'}
print (dic1)
=> {1: 'one', 2: 'two'}

dic1.clear()
print (dic1)
=> { }
```

del

Deletes the entire dictionary

[Example]

```
dic1 = {1: 'one', 2: 'two'}
del dic1
print (dic1)
=> NameError: name 'dic1' is not defined
```

get( )

Returns a value for the given key.
If the key is not found, it'll return the keyword None.
Alternatively, you can state the value to return if the key is not found.

[Example]

```
dic1 = {1: 'one', 2: 'two'}
dic1.get(1)
=> 'one'

dic1.get(5)
=> None

dic1.get(5, "Not Found")
=> 'Not Found'
```

in

Checks if an item is in a dictionary

[Example]

```
dic1 = {1: 'one', 2: 'two'}

# based on the key
1 in dic1
=> True

3 in dic1
=> False

# based on the value
'one' in dic1.values()
=> True

'three' in dic1.values()
=> False
```

items( )

Returns a list of dictionary's pairs as tuples

[Example]

```
dic1 = {1: 'one', 2: 'two'}
dic1.items()
=> dict_items([(1, 'one'), (2, 'two')])
```

keys( )

Returns list of the dictionary's keys

[Example]

```
dic1 = {1: 'one', 2: 'two'}
dic1.keys()
=> dict_keys([1, 2])
```

len( )

Find the number of items in a dictionary

[Example]

```
dic1 = {1: 'one', 2: 'two'}
print (len(dic1))
=> 2
```

update( )

Adds one dictionary's key-values pairs to another. Duplicates are removed.

[Example]

```
dic1 = {1: 'one', 2: 'two'}
dic2 = {1: 'one', 3: 'three'}

dic1.update(dic2)
```

```
print (dic1)
=> {1: 'one', 2: 'two', 3: 'three'}

print (dic2)    #no change
=> {1: 'one', 3: 'three'}
```

values( )

Returns list of the dictionary's values

[Example]

```
dic1 = {1: 'one', 2: 'two'}
dic1.values ()
=> dict_values(['one', 'two'])
```

Appendix E: Project Answers

Exercise 1.1

```
def printInstructions(instruction):
  print(instruction)
```

Exercise 1.2

```
def getUserScore(userName):
  try:
    input = open('userScores.txt', 'r')
    for line in input:
      content = line.split(', ')
      if content[0] == userName:
        input.close()
        return content[1]
    input.close()
    return '-1'
  except IOError:
    print("File not found. A new file will be
created.")
    input = open('userScores.txt', 'w')
    input.close()
    return '-1'
```

Exercise 1.3

```
def updateUserScore(newUser, userName, score):
  from os import remove, rename

  if newUser == True:
    input = open('userScores.txt', 'a')
    input.write(userName + ', ' + score + '\n')
    input.close()
  else:
    temp = open('userScores.tmp', 'w')
    input = open('userScores.txt', 'r')
```

```
    for line in input:
      content = line.split(', ')
      if content[0] == userName:
        temp.write(userName + ', ' + score +
'\n')
      else:
        temp.write(line)

    input.close()
    temp.close()

    remove('userScores.txt')
    rename('userScores.tmp', 'userScores.txt')
```

Exercise 2.1

```
class Game:
  def __init__(self, noOfQuestions = 0):
    self._noOfQuestions = noOfQuestions

  @property
  def noOfQuestions(self):
    return self._noOfQuestions

  @noOfQuestions.setter
  def noOfQuestions(self, value):
    if value < 1:
      self._noOfQuestions = 1
      print("\nMinimum Number of Questions = 1")
      print("Hence, number of questions will be
set to 1")
    elif value > 10:
      self._noOfQuestions = 10
      print("\nMaximum Number of Questions =
10")
      print("Hence, number of questions will be
set to 10")
    else:
```

```
        self._noOfQuestions = value
```

Exercise 2.2

```python
class BinaryGame(Game):
  def generateQuestions(self):
    from random import randint
    score = 0

    for i in range(self.noOfQuestions):
      base10 = randint(1, 100)
      userResult = input("\nPlease convert %d to
binary: " %(base10))
      while True:
        try:
          answer = int(userResult, base = 2)
          if answer == base10:
            print("Correct Answer!")
            score = score + 1
            break
          else:
            print("Wrong answer. The correct
answer is {:b}.".format(base10))
            break
        except:
          print("You did not enter a binary
number. Please try again.")
          userResult = input("\nPlease
convert %d to binary: " %(base10))

    return score
```

Exercise 2.3

```python
class MathGame(Game):
  def generateQuestions(self):
    from random import randint
    score = 0
```

```python
    numberList = [0, 0, 0, 0, 0]
    symbolList = ['', '', '', '']
    operatorDict = {1:' + ', 2:' - ', 3:'*',
4:'**'}

    for i in range(self.noOfQuestions):
      for index in range(0, 5):
        numberList[index] = randint(1, 9)
      #refer to explanation below
      for index in range(0, 4):
        if index > 0 and symbolList[index - 1]
== '**':
          symbolList[index] =
operatorDict[randint(1, 3)]
        else:
          symbolList[index] =
operatorDict[randint(1, 4)]

      questionString = str(numberList[0])

      for index in range(0, 4):
        questionString = questionString +
symbolList[index] + str(numberList[index+1])

      result = eval(questionString)

      questionString =
questionString.replace("**", "^")

      userResult = input("\nPlease evaluate %s:
"%(questionString))

      while True:
        try:
          answer = int(userResult)
          if answer == result:
            print("Correct Answer!")
            score = score + 1
```

```
                break
            else:
                print("Wrong answer. The correct
answer is {:d}.".format(result))
                break
        except:
            print("You did not enter a valid
number. Please try again.")
            userResult = input("\nPlease
evaluate %s: "%(questionString))

    return score

'''
Explanation

Starting from the second item (i.e. index = 1)
in symbolList, the line if index > 0 and
symbolList[index-1] == '**': checks if the
previous item in symbolList is the ** symbol.

If it is, the statement symbolList[index] =
operatorDict[randint(1, 3)] will execute. In
this case, the range given to the randint
function is from 1 to 3. Hence, the ** symbol,
which has a key of 4 in operatorDict  will NOT
be  assigned to symbolList[index].

On the other hand, if it is not, the statement
symbolList[index] = operatorDict[randint(1, 4)]
will execute. Since the range given to the
randint function is 1 to 4, the numbers 1, 2, 3
or 4 will be generated. Hence, the symbols +, -,
* or ** will be assigned to symbolList[index].

'''
```

Exercise 3.1

```
from gametasks import printInstructions,
getUserScore, updateUserScore
from gameclasses import Game, MathGame,
BinaryGame
```

Exercise 3.2

```
try:
  mathInstructions = '''
In this game, you will be given a simple
arithmetic question.
Each correct answer gives you one mark.
No mark is deducted for wrong answers.
'''

  binaryInstructions = '''
In this game, you will be given a number in base
10.
Your task is to convert this number to base 2.
Each correct answer gives you one mark.
No mark is deducted for wrong answers.
'''
  mg = MathGame()
  bg = BinaryGame()

  userName = input("\nPlease enter your
username: ")

  score = int(getUserScore(userName))

  if score == -1:
    newUser = True
    score = 0
  else:
    newUser = False
```

```python
  print("\nHello %s, welcome to the
game." %(userName))
  print("Your current score is %d." %(score))

  userChoice = 0

  while userChoice != '-1':
    game = input("\nMath Game (1) or Binary Game
(2)?: ")
    while game != '1' and game != '2':
      print("You did not enter a valid choice.
Please try again.")
      game = input("\nMath Game (1) or Binary
Game (2)?: ")

    numPrompt = input("\nHow many questions do
you want per game (1 to 10)?: ")
    while True:
      try:
        num = int(numPrompt)
        break
      except:
        print("You did not enter a valid number.
Please try again.")
        numPrompt = input("\nHow many questions
do you want per game (1 to 10)?: ")


    if game == '1':
      mg.noOfQuestions = num
      printInstructions(mathInstructions)
      score = score + mg.generateQuestions()
    else:
      bg.noOfQuestions = num
      printInstructions(binaryInstructions)
      score = score + bg.generateQuestions()
```

```python
    print("\nYour current score
is %d." %(score))

    userChoice = input("\nPress Enter to
continue or -1 to end: ")

    updateUserScore(newUser, userName, str(score))
```

Exercise 3.3

```python
except Exception as e:
  print("An unknown error occurred. Program will
exit.")
  print("Error: ", e)
```

Index

One Last Thing…

To me, programming is an art and a science. It is highly addictive and enjoyable. It is my hope to share this passion with as many people as possible.

If this guide has helped you, I would be deeply appreciative if you would take a few seconds to let your friends know about it.

In addition, I hope you do not stop learning here. If you are interested in more programming challenges, you can check out the site https://projecteuler.net/. Have fun!

Made in the USA
Lexington, KY
14 August 2019